WILDCATS TO POWERCATS

K-STATE FOOTBALL FACTS AND TRIVIA

MARK STALLARD

ADDAX
PUBLISHING
GROUP

Published by Addax Publishing Group, Inc.
Copyright © 2000 by Mark Stallard
Edited by John Dodderidge
Designed by Randy Breeden
Cover Designed by Laura Bolter

For Information address:
Addax Publishing Group, Inc.
8643 Hauser Drive, Suite 235, Lenexa, KS 66215

ISBN: 1-58497-004-9

Library of Congress Cataloging-in-Publication Data

Stallard, Mark, 1958-
    Wildcats to powercats : K-State football facts & trivia / by Mark Stallard.
        p. cm.
ISBN 1-58497-004-9
        1. Kansas State University--Football--Miscellanea. 2. Kansas State Wildcats
        (Football team)--Miscellanea. I. Title.

GV958.K35 S72 2000
796.332'63'0978128--dc 21
                                                                                    00-063938
Printed in the USA
1 3 5 7 9 10 8 6 4 2

ATTENTION: SCHOOLS AND BUSINESSES
Addax Publishing Group, Inc. books are available at quantity discounts with bulk
purchase for education, business, or sales promotional use. For information, please
write to: Special Sales Department, Addax Publishing Group, 8643 Hauser Drive,
Suite 235, Lenexa, Kansas 66215

This book is not an official publication of nor is it endorsed by Kansas State University.

Dedication

To my friend Larry Smith
and his life-long love for Kansas State University

"A lot of people consider it to be the biggest turnaround in college football history. To play under Coach Snyder and be a part of it is a tremendous feeling. At least you know you did something to make history."

- Kevin Lockett

Contents

WILDCATS

— TO —

POWERCATS

K-STATE FOOTBALL FACTS AND TRIVIA

Acknowledgments

It's been a long journey through the history of K-State football, and I want to extend my thanks to everyone who helped make it an enjoyable trip.

To Bob Snodgrass, my publisher, for making the book possible; to Michelle Washington, for displaying great patience with me; and to John Dodderidge for all his hard work and keen purple insight.

To everyone at the K-State Sports Information Office; Chet Savage, Andy Bartlett, and Krista Darting in particular. Their quick responses to my unending requests is greatly appreciated. Kent Brown and Craig Pinkerton also helped get me started.

To Dan Donnert, John LaBarge, Traci Bowman and Brenda Clark at KSU Photographic Services for providing me access to the great selection of K-State photos.

To Pat Patton and her excellent staff at the K-State Archives for supplying me with much needed information and photos.

To Barry Bunch and Ned Kehde at the University of Kansas Archives for providing several photos of K-State players and game action shots.

To my Mom and Dad, who searched for and found some important material for me.

To Mike Webber, who helped me ponder through the worthiness of some trivia questions, and expressed his much needed opinion on several items.

To my wonderful wife Merrie Jo for once again proving to me I couldn't write a book without her.

To the Kansas State football team and coaching staff, especially Coach Snyder. Your tremendous success is the reason for this book.

And finally, to the K-State fans. If ever one group of supporters deserved to have their emotional ties to a team rewarded, it is this large group of faithful, die-hard fans.

Introduction

A brutal 30-mile-per-hour wind from the north swept over KSU Stadium, stifling the players movements on the field, and rocking the spectators in the stands. The strong, never-ending gusts pushed back kicks and turned passes into wobbling ducks. The result was less than perfect football. But it was the 1972 K-State-KU game, and the mostly partisan Wildcat fans in the packed stadium didn't care. K-State was playing its top rival, and there was always the chance the Wildcats would beat the hated Jayhawks. Admittedly, these were two teams going nowhere – both were on probation, and between them they would win just seven games in the season. But this game was a good indication of what K-State football might be, and the kind of passion it could inspire throughout an entire season if the Wildcats fielded a more competitive team. As it was at the time, the K-State football crazies lived for the annual game against the Jayhawks, their expectations for each new season simple: beat KU, and it would be a somewhat successful year, no matter how many other games the team lost.

The Wildcats won that game in 1972, against the wind and KU, 20-19. With so few big wins to celebrate, the students did what they've done throughout the last 100 years when the Cats won an important game; they tore down the goal posts and set off a celebration across the campus to Aggieville.

This was my first taste of "Purple Pride" football, and the thing I remember most about this blustery game was the exuberance of the K-State fans. Their optimism wasn't reserved just for KU; Wildcat fans always believed they could pull off the miracle upset, as I saw many times later against such opponents as Nebraska and Oklahoma.

K-State's football fans had been long-suffering, and in the not-too-distant past, three or four wins in a season were considered a high-mark achievement. No more. The Wildcats regularly drub most of their opponents, and only Nebraska and Colorado have presented formidable challenges to the Wildcats since 1993. And consider this: It wasn't that long ago Wildcat fans were cheering the end of a 30-game winless streak. It isn't improbable to think they might someday be cheering a 30-game winning streak.

Kansas State's rise to the top of the college football world the past decade has been nothing short of extraordinary, but the Wildcats' assent wasn't a miracle. Great coaching, hard work, and a belief by the University that it could be a winner, could challenge Nebraska and other powerhouse teams in the country are what made the program a winner. Bill Snyder put together a plan for K-State football when he came to Manhattan in 1989, and he stuck to it. The results have been remarkable: Coach of the Year awards, All-American players, a No. 1 ranking in the polls, a top Heisman Trophy candidate, Academic All-Americans, a great stadium and facilities, and seven straight bowl games appearances.

But it wasn't magic, it wasn't a miracle.

Powercat logos are now everywhere in the state of Kansas, from Liberal to Overland Park, and Goodland to Independence. And they are also sprinkled across the country. K-State football is now synonymous with success, and K-Staters have relished the transition.

Wildcats to Powercats.

It's been a bumpy ride for K-State football fans, but the football program has arrived at an unparalleled level of success. With this in mind, if an event was of historical importance to the football team – good or bad – or important to the fans, I tried to include it in the book.

M.S.

Wildcat History

Coach Bill Snyder

Powercat Pride
A Brief Overview of K-State Football

From its beginning, K-State's football team struggled, and not for wins. The first couple years the game was played on campus and acceptance for the sport among the faculty and staff of the college was absent. They resisted the game and denied its popularity. But the students persisted, and by 1896 an organized, school-sponsored team became a permanent part of student life in Manhattan.

And then there was the losing.

The early days of college football in Kansas knew no "class" distinction among foes. Kansas State played almost every college in the state, and also played against some high school teams. They *lost* to high school teams. When Mike Ahearn took over the football coaching duties in 1905, many things changed and for the first time in the short history of K-State football, the team posted a winning record. Actually, K-State's football team was usually competitive throughout the first 40 years of the 20th century. It wasn't until just before World War II that the seemingly endless string of losing seasons started.

Coach after coach came to Manhattan, coach after coach was fired. The program was so bogged down with a losing mentality, it seemed at times to embrace the losers' role. More than 90 seasons of gridiron competition had yielded little success.

And then the football David turned into Goliath.

Bill Snyder's arrival at K-State marked the beginning of a new era in Kansas State's football fortunes, and the Wildcats shed their long-time doormat role.

They began to win football games. And then they won a lot of games.

Kansas State's football journey from Wildcats to Powercats has been a long one, much too long. Bill Snyder has shown that winning can become as much of a habit as losing ever was in the past. And as K-State zeros in on a national championship, it's a habit that should be hard to break.

Aggies

The Kansas State Athletic Department lists 1986 as the school's first official football season. The mascot "Aggies" was selected that year, as well as the school color of Royal Purple. Support to get the program started wasn't

15

Bill Snyder gets a victory shower following K-State's 52-17 win in the 1993 Copper Bowl.

easy, and as a result the K-State football team had trouble finding stability the first decade of its existence. The team won just 15 games in that time period.

But after nine consecutive seasons with nine different head coaches, K-State found a keeper in Mike Ahearn. Taking over the program in 1905, Ahearn led the Aggies to a 6-2 record. K-State never lost more than three games in a season under Ahearn, and in 1906 the school defeated the University of Kansas for the first time in five tries, winning 6-4 in Lawrence.

Bring on the Jayhawks

Their rivalry came naturally, and the animosities, fighting, bitterness and mutual dislike developed quickly.

Silo Tech versus Snob Hill.

From 1907 through the 1923 season, K-State could not defeat the Jayhawks. Each loss brought about another form of the "Jinx," a spell KU seemed to hold over K-State on the football field. Jayhawker fans reveled in their mastery over the Aggies, and each year at the start of the game would

16

The 1936 K-State – KU game.

yell "jinx, jinx," as the K-State team took the field. If KU didn't win by three or four touchdowns, a miracle play would occur to either secure a win or tie. Sometimes K-State would just play a horrible game.

By 1909, the intense animosity between the two institutions escalated to the point that they did not play one another in 1910.

After tying KU in 1922 and 1923, K-State finally went over the top in 1924 and defeated the Jayhawks, 6-0. This started a string of K-State dominance in the series that lasted until the end of the 1930s. KU again dominated in the series until the late 1960s when Vince Gibson's 1969 squad broke a 14-game winless streak against the Jayhawks, winning 26-22 in Lawrence. That was also the first season of the modern Governor's Cup Trophy, presented each season to the winner of the game.

Some great games in the series: K-State's 46-0 shellacking of KU in 1955, the 20-19 wind-blown K-State victory in 1972, K-State's dominating 36-20 win in 1978, the national TV massacre KSU put on the Jayhawks in 1982, the 1991 "Miracle in Manhattan" K-State win, the 21-13 Wildcat victory in Lawrence in 1994, and K-State's dominating performance over KU in 1995.

Bill Snyder and his teams have dominated the Jayhawks in recent years, winning seven in a row through the 1999 season, K-State's longest winning streak in the series. Snyder and crew have lost just three times to KU since he started coaching at K-State.

K-State fans prepare to tear down the goal posts after the Wildcats defeated KU at Lawrence in 1955.

Action from the 1955 K-State – KU game.

Elements of Perfection

The 1910 K-State football squad was the first great team at the school. Led by legendary coach Mike Ahearn, the Aggies compiled a 10-1 record. Unscored upon in their first six games, the Aggies lone loss of the season was to Colorado College, 15-8. Stars on the team included Captain George Croyle, Harvey Roots, Jack Holmes, Merle Simms and Horse Power Bates. This team defeated Drury College, 75-0, which is still the school record for the most points scored in a game.

Mike Ahearn resigned his coaching position following the season, and it would be 85 seasons before the Wildcats matched the 10 wins of the 1910 team.

Farmers and Wildcats

What's in a name? Kansas State changed the name of its mascot from Aggies to Wildcats in 1915 when John Bender took over as the football coach, because, he said, his squad had the fighting spirit of wildcats. Z. G. Clevenger changed the name again the following year when he became the head football coach, and K-State's mascot became the Farmers. When Charles Bachman arrived in 1920 to coach the team, he reverted back to Wildcats, which it's been ever since.

The 1910 K-State Aggies

Friendly Willie – 1954

Wildcat – 1970s

Beefed-up Willie – 1985

Fighting Wildcat – 1960s

Wildcat Logos

Starting in the early 1950s, K-State used Willie the Wildcat in various forms. When the Powercat logo became the official sports logo for K-State athletics, Willie was retired to the Alumni Association.

Wildcat cartoon in 1916 Royal Purple yearbook

A New Stadium

Combining the school's need for a new stadium with a way to honor the 45 K-State students who lost their lives in World War I, appropriation for the construction of Memorial Stadium was started in the spring of 1922. The

Memorial Stadium

west side of the stadium was ready the following fall, and the east side of the stadium was completed in 1924. Originally designed to be a horseshoe-shaped stadium, funding ran out at the onset of the Great Depression, and the stadium was not completed in its original design.

The Wildcats' first game at Memorial Stadium was on October 6, 1922, a 47-0 win over Washburn. The final game at Memorial Stadium was on November 18, 1967, a 40-6 loss to Colorado.

Conference Champs

Kansas State fielded several ͺ ͻd teams between 1924 and 1933, but the Wildcats always fell short of winning a conference title. After Bo McMillin left K-State, Lynn "Pappy" Waldorf was recruited from Oklahoma A&M to become the Wildcats' new coach. He was in Manhattan just one season, but oh, what a season. The Wildcats opened the season with a lackluster game against Fort Hays State, but won, 13-0. The team then earned a hard-fought tie with Manhattan (New York), but lost to Marquette. Kansas State then shut out the Jayhawks, but a loss to Tulsa put the team's record at 2-2-1. K-State won its final five games of the season, defeating Washburn, Missouri, Oklahoma, Iowa State, and on Thanksgiving, Nebraska. The Cats were a perfect 5-0 in the Big Six

"To show their appreciation to the newly crowned champions, the Manhattan Chamber of Commerce sponsored a huge banquet at the Wareham Ballroom. Gold footballs, emblematic of the conference championship, and large purple K blankets were presented to the team." – from the 1935 Royal Purple yearbook

The success didn't last. Waldorf moved on to Northwestern the following season, and his successor, Wes Fry, couldn't maintain the championship level of play. By 1940 the Wildcats were consistently playing losing football each season.

A Tradition of Losing

From 1940 through 1952, Kansas State won just 16 football games and went through six different head coaches (Hobbs Adams was the head coach in 1940-41 and 1946). At one point the school lost 28 straight games – K-State defeated Wichita in the first game of 1945 and didn't win again until the third game of the 1948 season. They were shut out 22 times between 1945 and 1952. The one bright spot in this string of losses was Harold Robinson, the first African-American to play football at K-State.

A Few Good Seasons

The losing was supposed to continue in 1953, but led by the outstanding talent of Veryl Switzer – a 1953 first team All-American – and Corky Taylor, Bill Meek's Wildcats put together a very good season, compiling a 6-3-1 record and second-place finish in the Big Seven.

The 1954 season proved to be even better for the Wildcats. Traveling to Boulder, Colorado, for the final game of the season, K-State needed a win to secure a spot in the Orange Bowl. The Wildcats couldn't handle the Buffaloes, though, and suffered a disappointing loss, 38-14. They ended the season with a 7-3 record.

The K-State sideline during a 1954 game.

Kansas State didn't have another winning season for 16 years.

"We Gonna Win"

Kansas State hired Vince Gibson to take over the football team in 1967, and his enthusiastic optimism for K-State was refreshing.

"I don't think K-State people realize what a great school they have and the potential it offers in the competitive area of college football," Gibson said shortly after taking the job in Manhattan. "... Now is the time when Kansas State can become a legend in the annals of collegiate football. We have something to sell: a great school, great people, and believe you me, physical facilities that in a short time will hold its own with any in the country." And he said one more thing, often and to anyone who would listen.

"We gonna win."

"Purple Pride" swept through the state, and Gibson began delivering on his word. K-State moved into KSU Stadium and won four games his second season at the helm. Lynn Dickey and Mack Herron provided an offensive firepower the Cats hadn't had in many seasons. The 1968 K-State team was ranked 20th in the nation after the first week of the season, and though the team finished at 4-6, it appeared the Wildcats were ready to become winners.

The 1969 team scored two major victories. For the first time in 14 seasons the Wildcats defeated KU.

Booming the Sooners

Of the great victories in the history of K-State football, the Wildcats stunning, dominant win over Oklahoma in 1969 has to be considered near the top. Winless against the Sooners for 34 years, Lynn Dickey led the Wildcats and had a fabulous game, completing 28 of 42 passes for 380 yards and three touchdowns. Mack Herron got into the end zone three times. K-State led 28-14 at the half and never looked back once the third quarter started.

"Oklahoma had the tradition, we've had nothin'," Gibson said after the game. "But we weren't awed by any tradition. We've had to build what we've got, but we've got confidence as a football team."

The win improved the Wildcats' record to 5-1, as well as moving them up to No. 12 in the polls.

The Oklahoma game was the last time K-State won in 1969, and the team dropped out of the Top 20 poll. Gibson and his team were ready for great things in the 1970 season, but during the week of the KU game, the bottom dropped out of Gibson's program.

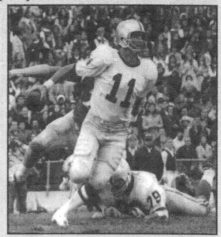

Lynn Dickey

Probation

On October 7, 1970, K-State's football team was placed on probation for three years by the Big Eight Conference. Violations were cited in four areas: financial aid, unethical conduct, scholastic eligibility and recruiting practices. Vince Gibson also received a formal reprimand. The killer was that K-State wouldn't be allowed to accept a bowl bid, nor would it be allowed on TV for the full three-year period.

Gibson always blamed KU for the probation (the Jayhawks received a two-year probation on the same day as the Wildcats), but the newspaper accounts of the day also cited Missouri as a possibility for turning in the Wildcats. Either way it didn't matter.

"At one time, I tell you what, he (Pepper Rodgers, KU's coach in 1970) killed my program," Gibson said of the strict penalties assessed K-State. "He hurt my whole coaching career."

Vince Gibson (right) and KU coach Pepper Rodgers

Reverting to Old Ways

Vince Gibson could never revive his team from the depths of the harsh probation, and after winning just four games in 1974, he left K-State to coach at Louisville. Two years later K-State was again at the bottom of the heap in college football, and finished with a 1-10 record.

Ellis Rainsberger, a standout player for KSU in the 1950s, took over the head coaching position in 1975, but won only six games in three seasons. Like so many times in the past, K-State was forced to start over.

Bowl Dreams do Come True

Jim Dickey had a plan.

He wanted to redshirt his 1981 senior class to give them an extra year of maturity, an extra year to grow stronger. The hope was that an abundance of fifth-year players would dramatically improve K-State's position in the Big Eight, giving the team a realistic shot at competing for a bowl.

Jim Dickey (center) enjoys a good moment during the 1982 season.

The seniors followed the coach's plan and sat down for the 1981 season. The bad part of the payoff was the lack of talent on the 1981 team, and the Wildcats finished 2-9 that year. But the seniors returned the following season, and as if it were written to script, produced the best season K-State had had since 1954, and earned the school's first-ever bowl bid.

K-State lost the 1982 Independence Bowl to Wisconsin, and the follow-

KSU Stadium in 1995

ing season Dickey watched as his team slid back to a 3-8 record. Two games into the 1985 season, Dickey resigned as K-State's football coach.

30 Games, 29 Losses, One Tie

"I told him it was the toughest Division 1-A job in America," former KSU Athletic Director Steve Miller said. "Don't let anyone kid you about that. Is it a hard job? It's not a hard job; it's the hardest job in this country."

The man who took the "hard" job was Bill Snyder. The persona of the football team changed immediately; Snyder wasn't interested in just winning football games, he was interested in winning, period. And everything that goes with it. He wanted a new logo for the football team and got it, a logo that became so popular that the entire university adopted it.

His first team won just one game, but never has one victory been so symbolic. K-State defeated North Texas State on September 30, 1989, ending a 30-game winless streak. The climb to the top of the football mountain had started.

Wildcats to Powercats

K-State got progressively better in each of Snyder's first four seasons, but

The 1998 Kansas State Wildcats

The goal posts come down after K-State defeats Nebraska in 1998, 40-30.

the team had yet to make the step into a bowl game. 1993 ended the wait, and when the Wildcats throttled Wyoming in the Copper Bowl to finish with a 9-2-1 record, K-State had its best team since 1910. K-State won 10 games in 1995, and the 1997 team became the first in the school's history to win 11 games.

K-State was ready to challenge for the national title in 1998. Senior quarterback Michael Bishop was a threat running or throwing, and he was one of those rare players who could control a game by himself. The Wildcats breezed through the first nine games on their schedule, and had earned a No. 1 ranking in the ESPN/USA Today coaches poll. Only Nebraska, it seemed, stood in the way of K-State and a shot at the national championship.

The Cornhuskers had defeated K-State 29 straight times, but on November 14, 1998, K-State finally got past Nebraska and won, 40-30. It was the most important win in the history of the football program; the Wildcats clinched a spot in the Big 12 Championship game, and also put them in position to play for the national title.

Texas A&M destroyed the title hopes K-State had, though, defeating

Joe Bob Clements celebrates during 1998 Nebraska game.

them in the Big 12 Championship game in St. Louis in double overtime. This one game might be the hardest loss suffered by the school. The Wildcats never fully recovered from the A&M game, and also fell in the Alamo Bowl to Purdue. But 1999 saw the Wildcats rebound from the tough losses to win 11 games for the third straight season. They defeated Washington in the Holiday Bowl.

Bill Snyder has built a tremendous football program at K-State. The challenge of winning a national title will always be within range of his pursuit.

Michael Bishop struggles for extra yardage against Nebraska in the 1998 game.

K-State Football Chronology

The early days of Kansas State football saw the team play high schools and small colleges. Football was considered somewhat barbaric in the 1890s, and the college was apprehensive and slow to support the sport. By 1900 the school had a complete schedule of games and football was extremely popular. Still, many traditions and rivalries started slowly – K-State and KU didn't play until 1902 – and the Aggies didn't start playing in a conference until 1913. Most of the dates in this chronology highlight great moments in the history of Kansas State football, as well as the disappointments.

1892

December 2 - *The Industrialist* (the school's weekly paper) reported in its December 3 edition Kansas State Agricultural College's (KSAC) first football game. "An interesting game of football between the first- and second-year teams was witnessed by a large number of students at the city park." The report gives the players names and positions played of the two teams, and the score was 4 to 4. Sophomore Arthur D. Benson from Colfax, Illinois, who played "quarter back" in the game, was responsible for spawning interest in the sport to his classmates in 1891.

For the next four to five years the College faculty and administration struggle with the concept of a football team for the school.

1893

November 23 - The first out-of-town game authorized by the faculty. A group of students and faculty traveled to St. Mary's Academy for this game, which the KSAC team won, 18-10.

1894 gridsters – KSAC's first football team.

1894

November 3 - A team representing KSAC, with the permission of the faculty, loses to a town team in Abilene, Kansas, 24-0.

1885

St. Mary's, Kansas, challenges KSAC to a football game, but the college declines because they didn't have a team.

1896

This season is considered the first in Kansas State's football history. The squad was coached by Ira Pratt (the school's first coach), and the nickname "Aggies" was selected, as well as the school's official color of Royal Purple.

November 28 - The Aggies travel to Junction City and play a squad of soldiers from Fort Riley on Thanksgiving Day. The soldiers prevail, 14-0.

December 5 - The Fort Riley team comes to Manhattan and this time the Aggies forge a tie, 6-6. KSAC's first official season ends with a record of 0-1-1.

1897

Fall - The city of Manhattan grants the use of the public square bounded by Eighth and Vattier Streets and Bluemont and Juliett Avenues for use as an athletic field for KSAC. Football games were played on this field starting with the 1897 season.

November 1 - KSAC wins its first-ever football game, defeating Chapman High School, 4-0, in Manhattan.

November 20 - The Aggies travel to Topeka and are handily beaten by Washburn University, 36-0. KSAC ends the season with a record of 1-2-1.

1898

November 5 - The Aggies defeat Junction City High School, 26-0.

November 28 - Ottawa University beats KSAC, 16-6. The Aggies finish the season with a 1-1-2 record.

1899

October 14 - Washburn blanks the Aggies in Topeka, 24-0.

October 30 - KSAC defeats Kansas Wesleyan in Manhattan, 17-5. This was the Aggies' first win ever over a college team opponent.

November 30 - KSTC-Emporia defeats KSAC, 20-0. The Aggies finish the season with 2-3 record.

1900

October 22 - Fairmount College (now Wichita State) falls to the Aggies in Wichita, 11-5.

November 17 - The Aggies slap a rout on Kansas Wesleyan, easily defeating them, 30-0.

November 30 - KSAC closes out the season with a loss at St. Mary's, 28-6. The team finishes with a 2-4 record.

The 1900 KSAC football team

1901

May - A roofed grandstand is added to the athletic field.

October 7 - KSAC opens the season with a 12-5 win at Bethany.

October 14 - The Aggies shut out the College of Emporia in Manhattan, 11-0.

November 20 - The Aggies overwhelm Manhattan High School with an easy 30-0 win.

December 1 - Washington (Kansas) High School forges a tie with KSAC, 6-6. The Aggies finish the season with three wins, four losses and a tie.

1902

September 27 - KSAC travels to Emporia and loses to KSTC, 16-0.

October 4 - Because of heavy rain and a sloppy field, the Aggies' game with KU in Lawrence is postponed.

October 7 - Bring on the Jayhawkers. The Aggies travel to Lawrence and play KU for the first time. Though defeated 16-0, the Agricultural College played tough on defense and held the Jayhawkers to a much lower score than anticipated. Of note, Dr. James Naismith, the inventor of basketball, was one of the timekeepers for the game.

For the visitors (KSAC) Briggs, the plucky quarter, played a star game, even after he was crippled, while Nelson, at fullback, and Towne, the captain and right half, showed themselves to be great players. Towne was in every play, broke the Kansas line time and again and always helped his man advance the ball ... The score was not as large as Kansas had hoped to make it.

- From the account of the first game between KU and K-State as reported in the *Kansas City Times*, October 8, 1902

November 10 - Bethany smothers the Aggies, 40-0.

November 27 - KSAC concludes the season with a 22-5 win over Chapman High School. The Aggies finish with a record of 2-6.

1903

October 3 - The Aggies travel to Lawrence and are shut out by the Jayhawkers, 34-0.

October 30 - KSAC defeats Clyde High School, 11-0. This is the last time the Aggies play a high school opponent.

November 26 - Haskell Institute comes to Manhattan and loses big to the Aggies, 34-6. KSAC finishes the season with a 3-4-1 record.

1904

October 8 - KSAC wins an easy victory over Fort Riley, 28-0.

October 31 - Fort Hays State comes to Manhattan and shuts out the Aggies, 17-0.

November 12 - Washburn embarrasses the Aggies in Topeka, 56-0.

November 18 - Once again the Aggies fall to the Jayhawkers, this time by a score of 41-4. However, this game marked the first time KSAC scored on its in-state rival. Walter Scholz kicked a field goal to produce the points.

November 24 - KSTC-Emporia defeats KSAC in the final game of the season, 34-6. The Aggies finish with a record of 1-6.

1905

After nine different coaches through its first nine seasons, the football program finds stability when Mike Ahearn takes over the coaching duties.

October 7 - The Ahearn era starts with a win over Ottawa at home, 20-0.

October 14 - Washburn defeats KSAC in Manhattan, 12-5.

The 1905 KSAC Aggies

October 31 - The Aggies down Fairmount College (Wichita) in Manhattan, 11-6.

November 25 - Once the Aggies fall to KU, this time by a score of 28-0 in Lawrence.

November 30 - KSAC ends a very good season with a strong performance, downing KSTC-Emporia, 10-0. The team finishes with a 6-2 record, the best-ever to date for the Aggies.

1906

Spring - A new grandstand is added to the athletic field. A small building is also added, to be used as a dressing room and for baths.

October 13 - The Aggies start the season with a 10-5 victory over Haskell.

October 22 - KSAC crushes the College of Emporia in Manhattan, 35-0.

October 27 - Washburn squeaks out a close win over the Aggies in Topeka, 5-4.

Mike Ahearn

November 23 - Manhattan celebrates! The Aggies down the Jayhawkers for the first time ever, defeating Kansas in Lawrence, 6-4. Aggie Carl Mallon, the team's captain, picked off a blocked Kansas kick in midair and raced 55 yards for the game's only touchdown. He also kicked the extra point. "Our men were overconfident and didn't realize what a stiff proposition they were up against," KU's coach Bert Kennedy said after the game. "The Manhattan boys played with ... desperate fighting spirit ..." At halftime, approximately 1,000 Aggie rooters paraded the football field, yelling and screaming rabid support for their team.

November 29 - The Aggies finish the season with a 10-0 win over KSTC-Emporia. KSAC finishes the season with a record of 5-2.

1907

Spring - Spring practice is conducted for the first time. Also, white sweaters with a block letter purple "K" are presented to players who played in a sufficient number of games.

October 7 - The Aggies start the season by putting an embarrassing whipping on the team from the College of Emporia, 46-0.

> *The victory of the College over the State University on the gridiron yesterday brought forth an enthusiasm among our students and citizens that was without parallel in the history of the institution; all the more because it had been a clean game from start to finish. The streets were thronged in the evening with shouting students, a bonfire was lighted, and the College bell rang, speeches were made-all felt that it was a famous victory.*
> *- From the account of the Aggies' 1906 win over KU in* The Industrialist.

October 19 - KSAC easily handled the K. C. Veterinarians in Manhattan, winning 32-0.

October 26 - Kansas exacted a little revenge from the previous season's defeat and downed the Aggies in Lawrence, 29-10.

November 28 - K-State wrapped up a 5-3 season by defeating KSTC-Emporia at home, 21-0.

1908

January - The Board of Regents limit away football games to no more than five per season.

The Athletic Association provided a training table to the players for the first time. Coach Ahearn was pleased with the results as most of the men gained a significant amount of weight.

October 3 - Kansas Wesleyan falls to the Aggies in Manhattan, 28-5.

October 10 - KU defeats K-State in Lawrence, 12-6.

October 28 - KSAC blanks Southwestern in Manhattan, 17-0.

November 7 - For the first in the history of the football program, the Aggies travel outside the state of Kansas. The trip is a good one as the team defeats Creighton in Omaha, 13-0.

November 14 - The Aggies stuff their counterparts from Oklahoma, defeating Oklahoma A&M 40-10 in Manhattan.

November 21 - A good trip to Topeka. KSAC defeats Washburn for the first time, 23-4. A full day's vacation was allowed to the students at the College to celebrate the broken "Hoodoo" of Washburn.

November 26 - The Aggies finish another good season with a win against Colorado College at home, 33-10. KSAC finishes with a record of 6-2.

1909

October 2 - The Aggies start the season with a rousing win over Kansas Wesleyan, 35-0.

October 9 - The Aggies travel to Columbia, Missouri, and play the Tigers for the first time. The outcome is a disappointment, though, as Mizzou wins, 3-0, in a hard-fought game.

October 16 - The Aggies lose a highly competitive game to the Kansas Jayhawkers, 5-3, in Manhattan. A dispute over the game causes a rift between the two schools, and they do not schedule a game for 1910.

October 23 - Southwestern is crushed by KSAC, 60-0.

November 6 - Creighton comes to Manhattan and goes home soundly beaten. The Aggies pound on the Omaha school, 58-3.

November 20 - Fairmount College (Wichita) takes a tremendous beating from the Aggies, 71-0.

November 25 - The Aggies finish the year in style, waxing Washburn in Topeka, 40-0. K-State finishes with a 7-2 record.

1910

March 24 - The Board of Regents votes to build a stadium on the southwest corner of the campus.

September 28 - The Aggies start one of the school's greatest seasons ever by pounding William Jewell, 57-0.

October 1 - Haskell is another easy victim for KSAC. The Aggies win, 39-0, in Manhattan.

October 17 - The Aggies score a school record 75 points against Drury as they coast to an overwhelming victory, 75-5.

November 5 - Colorado College spoils the Aggies' bid for a perfect season and defeats K-State, 15-8.

November 24 - KSAC finishes a great 10-1 season with a resounding 33-0 win over Washburn in Manhattan. The stars on this powerful team were Captain George Croyle, Harvey Roots, Jack Holmes and Merle Simms. This game also marked the end of Mike Ahearn's coaching career; he finished with an overall record of 39-12.

> *From the bottom of our left ventrical (sic) we utter the declaration that the football machine of 1910 has embodied in it more of the elements of perfection than any of its predecessors. A machine that could participate in eleven melees, and in only one fail to deliver the necessary energy, must have a very low coefficient of friction and a multitude of interchangeable parts.*
>
> *- From the 1911 Royal Purple Yearbook*

1911

Guy Lowman took over as the head coach of the K-State football team. The school also began the application process to join the Missouri Valley Conference, and played its first games on the new athletic field.

September 30 - The Aggies forge a 6-6 tie with Southwestern in Lowman's first game as KSAC's head man.

October 28 - Fairmount College falls to K-State in Manhattan, 9-5.

November 18 - The Aggies travel to Kansas City and defeat Arkansas, 3-0. A dropkick by halfback L.L. Howenstine in the third quarter provided the margin of victory at Kansas City's Gordon-Koppel Athletic Field.

November 30 - KSAC squeezes out a tight 6-5 win over Washburn in Topeka and finishes the season with a 5-4-1 record.

Action from the 1912 KSAC – KU game.

1912

October 5 - The Aggies pick up their second win of the season by stopping Haskell at home, 21-14.

October 25 - KSAC falls to Kansas again. "To the strains of minstrel music ringing on the K.U. field, the Aggies went down, before the University of

Kansas in the hardest defeat of the year," the *Royal Purple's* report of the game reads. "The score, 19 to 6, in no way indicates the closeness of the game. Time and again Aggie rooters were brought to their feet by spectacular plays that looked for the instant like victory for the Purple and White."

November 2 - The Aggies slaughter Fairmount College in Wichita, 54-0.

November 20 - KSAC travels to Texas and defeats Texas A&M in a close game, 13-10.

November 28 - K-State wraps up another successful season with a 21-3 victory over Washburn at home. The Aggies close with an 8-2 record.

1913

The Aggies begin play in the Missouri Valley Conference.

October 3 - KSAC drops the season opener to Southwestern, 13-10.

November 1 - Fairmount College provides an easy victory for the Aggies. KSAC wins at home, 30-7.

November 27 - KSAC finishes the season with a Thanksgiving Day game against Washburn in Topeka. The game ends in a 6-6 tie, and Aggies end up with a record of 3-4-1 for the season, 0-2 in the conference.

1914

October 3 - The Aggies open the season with a 15-10 win over Southwestern in Manhattan.

October 24 - Kansas throws a shutout at KSAC, winning 28-0 in Lawrence.

November 13 - The Oklahoma Sooners pound the Aggies in Manhattan, 52-10.

November 25 - Washburn wins against K-State in Manhattan, 26-16. The loss leaves the Aggies with a 1-5-1 record, 0-3 and last place in the MVC.

1915

John "Chief" Bender takes over the head coaching duties for KSAC. The team's mascot name is officially changed from "Aggies" to "Wildcats."

October 1 - KSAC starts the year with a 9-0 win over Southwestern.

October 23 - K-State's first Homecoming Game. Kansas comes to Manhattan and ruins the Wildcats' initial Homecoming game and wins, 19-7.

October 29 - The Wildcats travel to Columbia and fight Missouri to a 0-0 tie.

November 6 - KSAC defeats Friends, 14-0.

November 12 - The Wildcats defeat Washburn in Topeka, 6-0.

November 19 - Oklahoma defeats KSAC in Manhattan, 21-7. The Wildcats end the season with a record of 3-4-1.

1916

Z. G. Clevenger is the new head coach for KSAC. The mascot name is changed again, this time to "Farmers."

> ### The First Homecoming Game
> *To honor former football players and bring back old alumni, KSAC's coach John Bender organized the first Homecoming game at the College in 1915. His motivation behind the event was simple: he wanted to instill a winning attitude into his players. The 1916 Royal Purple said of that first Homecoming: "If there was ever any doubt in the minds of the students as to the loyalty of the Old Grads to K.S.A.C., it was banished last fall when the Alumni came in from all parts of the country, in response to an invitation to come and help celebrate the First Annual Homecoming Day." Homecoming became an annual event (although it was skipped a few times), but regardless of the other festivities that have become connected with it, football has always been the centerpiece for the day.*

September 30 - The Farmers shut out Baker to open the season, winning 20-0.

October 28 - The Farmers fight the Jayhawks to a 0-0 tie in Lawrence.

November 17 - KSAC squeaks out a 14-13 win over Oklahoma.

November 23 - The Farmers close out the season with an explosion on offense and trounce Washburn, 47-0. KSAC finishes the season with an impressive 6-1-1 record.

December 7 - The football field is graded and drainage tiles are installed by the student body and faculty of the college.

1917

September 29 - KSAC throws another shutout on Baker, winning 28-0.

October 20 - The Farmers travel to St. Louis and destroy Washington, 61-0.

November 3 - The Jayhawks defeat KSAC in Manhattan, 9-0.

November 29 - The Farmers close out the season with a 38-0 win over Washburn. Their record for the season is 6-2.

1918

The 1918 season was shortened dramatically because of World War I and the influenza epidemic.

September 27 - Once again the Farmers shut out Baker and win at home, 22-0.

November 23 - KSAC defeats Iowa State, 11-0.

November 28 - Kansas ruins the Farmers' chance at an undefeated season and win a tight game in Lawrence, 13-7. KSAC finishes the shortened campaign with a 4-1 record.

1919

September 27 - For the fourth year in a row the Farmers begin the season by shutting out Baker, 16-0.

October 24 - KSAC defeats Fort Hays State, 12-0.

November 26 - The Oklahoma Sooners stop the Farmers in Manhattan, 14-3. KSAC ends the season with a record of 3-5-1.

1920

Charles Bachman becomes the head coach of KSAC's football team. The team's nickname is changed for the last time, back to Wildcats.

October 1 - Fort Hays State loses to the Wildcats in Manhattan, 14-0.

October 22 - The Wildcats travel to Omaha and defeat Creighton, 3-0.

November 19 - KSAC fights the Sooners to a 7-7 tie.

November 26 - Washburn comes to Manhattan and surprises the Wildcats and forges a tie, 0-0. The team finishes with a 3-3-3 record.

1921

October 8 - The Wildcats stop Washington (St. Louis) at home, 21-0.

October 22 - KSAC defeats Missouri in Manhattan, 7-5.

October 21 - The Sooners lose to the Wildcats, 14-7. KSAC finishes the year with a 5-3 record.

1922

October 6 - The first game at Memorial Stadium. Only three wings of the stadium were completed. The Wildcats open the season in their new home (actually new stands on their old field) by stomping Washburn, 47-0.

October 28 - The Jayhawks come to Manhattan for the Wildcats' Homecoming game and are lucky to leave with a tie, 7-7. Ray Hahn scored on a 70-yard interception return for the Wildcats' touchdown.

November 2 - The Wildcats drop Mizzou in Columbia, 14-10. Arthur Stark and Maurice Sears scored touchdowns for KSAC.

November 30 - KSAC thrashes Texas Christian at home, 45-0, scoring all its points in the second half. The Wildcats end another good year, posting a 5-1-2 record.

1923

October 5 - The Wildcats start the season with a strong 25-0 win over Washburn at Memorial Stadium.

October 27 - For the second season in a row the Wildcats and Jayhawks fight to a tie, 0-0. KSAC outplayed KU in every aspect of the game, but could not score. The Wildcats had 320 yards of total offense, KU just 75.

November 3 - Mizzou ruins Homecoming, beating the Wildcats, 4-2.

November 23 - KSAC scores a tight win over the Sooners, defeating Oklahoma 21-20 in Manhattan. More than 8,000 fans showed up for the game.

November 30 - The season ends with a 34-12 loss at Nebraska. KSAC is 4-2-2 for the year.

1924

The east side of Memorial Stadium is completed. Plans to add seats in the south end zone, making the stadium a horseshoe, are never completed.

October 3 - The Wildcats defeat Washburn 23-0 to start the 1924 season. John Mildrexter scored twice for KSAC in the game.

KSAC and KU before their 1924 battle. The Wildcats were victorious, 6-0.

October 18 - It's over! The Wildcats end the Jayhawk jinx and defeat Kansas for the first time since 1906, 6-0.

November 22 - Nebraska spoils Homecoming, defeating the Wildcats, 24-0.

November 26 - The season ends with KSAC and Oklahoma fighting to a tie, 7-7. The Wildcats dominated the game, outgaining the Sooners 232 yards to 113, but couldn't get the tie-breaking score to win. The Wildcats finish with a mark of 3-4-1.

1925

October 3 - The Wildcats shut out the Sooners, 16-0.

October 17 - KSAC beats the Jayhawks, 14-7.

Breaking the Jayhawk Jinx

Winless against their top rival since 1906, the Wildcats put an end to the so-called "Jayhawk jinx" in 1924, and finally defeated KU, 6-0. K-State's Donald Meek raced 67 yards with a recovered fumble for the game's only touchdown. KU made several attempts to score throughout the second half, but the Wildcats were not to be denied victory this time.

Since KSAC's lone victory in 1906, the Wildcats had found a series of ways to lose to KU. By the 1910s, obnoxious KU students and fans had become so accustomed to "fate" handing them a win against KSAC that they would yell "jinx, jinx!" when the Wildcats took the field at the beginning of games. With the win in 1924, KSAC begin a run of dominance in the series that lasted almost 20 years.

November 14 - The Wildcats and Cornhuskers fight to a 0-0 tie at KSAC's Homecoming game.

November 19 - Iowa State falls to the Wildcats, 12-7. KSAC posts a 5-2-1 record for the year.

1926

October 2 - The Wildcats start the season with a solid win over the Texas Longhorns, 13-3.

October 16 - The Wildcats embarrass KU in Manhattan, 27-0. KSAC's Joe Holsinger scored on a short pass play, Elwin Feather had a 43-yard touchdown run and James Douglas rambled in from 24 yards out. The Wildcats' defense held KU to just three first downs and 76 yards of offense.

November 13 - KSAC drops a heartbreaker to Nebraska, 3-0.

November 26 - Iowa State squeaks past the Wildcats, 3-2. After winning its first five games of the season, KSAC loses three in a row to finish at 5-3.

1927

September 24 - K-State scores an easy win over Fort Hays State to start the season, 30-6.

October 15 - The Wildcats defeat Kansas for the fourth straight year, stopping the Jayhawks in Lawrence, 13-2.

November 24 - KSAC loses to Oklahoma A&M, 25-18, and finish the year with a 3-5 mark.

Charles Bachman concludes his career as K-State's head coach, finishing with an overall record of 33-23-9.

1928

A. N. "Bo" McMillin becomes the head football coach at KSAC.

September 29 - Bo McMillin begins his K-State coaching career with a win as the Wildcats easily beat Bethany, 32-7.

The 1928 K-State Wildcats

October 6 - KSAC stops Oklahoma A&M in Stillwater, 13-6.

October 20 - Kansas drops the Wildcats for the first time since 1921, winning 7-0 in Manhattan.

November 29 - KSAC ends the season with an 8-0 loss to Nebraska. McMillin's squad finishes with a 3-5 record.

1929

October 19 - The Wildcats shut out the Jayhawks in Lawrence, 6-0. A "triple pass" play for 50 yards set up K-State's touchdown, which was scored by George Wiggins.

October 26 - The Sooners sneak past KSAC and spoil Homecoming, 14-13.

November 2 - Another close game, and this time K-State wins. Missouri falls to the Wildcats, 7-6. George Wiggins intercepted a pass and ran 85 yards for K-State's touchdown, and C. O. Tackwell kick the extra point that proved to be the game-winning point.

November 28 - Marquette defeats K-State, 25-6, in the final game of the season. The Wildcats stand at 3-5 for the year.

1930

October 4 - Washburn falls to KSAC in Manhattan to start the new season, 14-0.

October 18 - Kansas defeats the Wildcats, 14-0.

November 15 - KSAC shuts out the Cyclones in Ames, winning 13-0.

November 27 - The Wildcats end the season on a high note, defeating Nebraska in Lincoln, 10-9. The team's record for the year is 5-3.

1931

The name of the school is officially changed to Kansas State College of Agriculture and Applied Science.

October 3 - KSAC begins one of the school's best seasons with a 28-7 win over KSTC-Pittsburg.

October 17 - The Wildcats celebrate Homecoming with a 13-0 win over Kansas.

October 24 - The Sooners can't handle K-State; the Wildcats defeat Oklahoma in Manhattan, 14-0.

November 7 - K-State loses a tough one to Iowa State, 7-6.

December 5 - K-State finishes the season with a 20-6 win over the Wichita Wheatshockers in a charity game in Wichita. Ralph Graham scored two touchdowns for the Wildcats. About $5,500 was raised from the proceeds of the game. The win put the Wildcats' season mark at 8-2.

1932

September 24 - The Wildcats start the season with a win over Wichita at Memorial Stadium, 26-0.

October 7 - Kansas State plays its first-ever night game. The Wildcats take on Kansas Wesleyan under the lights in Salina. It's an easy win for K-State, 52-6.

October 15 - Missouri falls to K-State, 25-0.

November 5 - Kansas State shuts out the Cyclones, 31-0.

November 19 - The Wildcats are upset by Kansas, losing 19-0 in Manhattan. K-State finishes the season with a 4-4 record.

1933

September 30 - K-State toys with KSTC-Emporia, winning handily, 25-0.

October 9 - Nebraska wins K-State's Homecoming game, 9-0.

October 28 - K-State wins a tough game against the Jayhawks in Lawrence, 6-0. A long pass from Lee Morgan to Ohen Stoner in the third quarter provided the winning score for the Wildcats.

November 18 - The Wildcats run wild over the Sooners. Dougal Russell gains 150 yards rushing and scores two touchdowns. Ralph Graham also has a big day and picks up 115 yards on the ground. K-State beats Oklahoma, 14-0.

November 30 - The Wildcats travel to Lubbock, Texas, and lose to Texas Tech, 6-0. K-State finishes the season with a record of 6-2-1. This game marked the end of Bo McMillin's coaching stint at K-State. He compiled an overall record of 29-21-1 in six seasons.

1934

Lynn "Pappy" Waldorf becomes K-State's new head football coach.

October 6 - The Wildcats fight to a tough, hard-earned tie with Manhattan College in New York, 13-13.

1934 Big Six Champs

October 20 - Homecoming is a success as the Wildcats shut down KU and win, 13-0.

November 17 - K-State steals one from the Sooners in Norman, winning 8-7.

November 24 - Iowa State can't handle the Wildcat defense and is shut out by K-State, 20-0.

November 29 - Big Six Champs! K-State disappointed a Thanksgiving Day crowd of 22,000 in Lincoln, Nebraska, and won the Big Six Championship over the Cornhuskers, 19-7. Oren Stoner was the star for the Purple-clad Kansans, scoring two touchdowns. The victory put K-State's conference record at 5-0, and 7-2-1 for the season.

K-State and Nebraska fight for the Big Six Championship in 1934. K-State won the game and the title, 19-7.

1935

Pappy Waldorf leaves K-State for Northwestern, and Wes Fry takes over the head coaching position.

September 27 - The Wildcats start the season with a 12-0 win over Duquesne.

October 19 - Nebraska comes to Manhattan and forges a 0-0 tie with K-State.

October 26 - The Jayhawks surprise Kansas State and win, 9-2.

November 9 - The Wildcats defeat Iowa State, 6-0.

November 23 - K-State and Missouri finish the season with a 7-7 tie. The Wildcats post a 2-4-3 record for the season.

1936

September 26 - Kansas State starts the new season with a 13-0 win over Fort Hays State.

October 24 - Homecoming feathers. K-State easily disposes of the KU Jayhawks at Homecoming, 26-6.

The Wildcats advance the ball against KU during the 1936 Homecoming game.

November 7 - K-State and Oklahoma fight to a 6-6 tie. Red Elder returns a kickoff 74 yards for the Wildcats' only touchdown in the game.

November 14 - Kansas State slaughters Iowa State in Manhattan, 47-7.

November 21 - The 13th-ranked Nebraska Cornhuskers blank the Wildcats in the season finale, 40-0. K-State finishes with a 4-3-2 record.

1937

October 16 - Marquette is K-State's first victim of the season, losing in Manhattan, 13-0. The Wildcats' record is 1-2.

November 13 - K-State travels to Lawrence and brings home a win over the Jayhawks, 7-0.

November 27 - The 11th-ranked Cornhuskers have all they can handle in the Wildcats, but leave Manhattan with a 3-0 win. K-State ends the season with a 4-5 mark.

Elmer Hackney fights off KU tacklers in 1937.

1938

October 1 - K-State loses to Northwestern in Chicago, 21-0.

October 29 - Kansas overpowers the Wildcats and spoils the Homecoming festivities, winning 27-7.

November 5 - K-State loses to the 11th-ranked Oklahoma Sooners, 26-0.

November 12 - Iowa State scores twice in the final five minutes of the game and gains a tie with K-State, 13-13. Elmer Hackney led the Wildcats with a touchdown run, and Melvin Seelye hauled in a touchdown pass.

November 19 - K-State wallops Washburn, 41-14. Elmer Hackney scored twice, and Melvin Seelye and Art Kirk also added touchdowns for the Wildcats.

November 24 - Nebraska beats K-State, 14-7. The Wildcats conclude the year with a 4-4-1 record.

1939

September 30 - K-State opens the season with a resounding 34-7 win over Fort Hays State at Memorial Stadium.

October 6 - The Wildcats defeat Marquette, 3-0.

October 28 - For the second time ever in the history of television, a football game is televised, and the game is Kansas State and 10th-ranked Nebraska. It's also Homecoming in Manhattan, but the Cornhuskers spoil everything by winning, 25-9.

November 4 - K-State runs over the Jayhawks in Lawrence, winning in convincing fashion by a 27-6 score.

November 11 - Sixth-ranked Oklahoma has all it can handle in K-State and escapes with a 13-10 win in Manhattan.

November 25 - Boston College puts a 38-7 defeat on the Wildcats, who finish the year with a 4-5 record. The game is also the last of Wes Fry's career. He concludes his time as the Wildcats' head man with a 18-21-6 overall record.

1940

Hobbs Adams is named as the head coach of the Wildcats.

September 28 - The Wildcats defeat KSTC-Emporia in Manhattan, 21-16.

The Peace Pact Trophy
In an effort to subdue the clashing student bodies of KU and K-State during their football contests, the student councils of the two rival schools purchased a "Peace Pact" Trophy to be presented to the winning team each year following the game. The trophy was bronze miniature goal posts, and it was hoped the winning team's student body would refrain from tearing down the loser's goal posts after the game.

October 26 - Homecoming is a success as the Wildcats defeat the Jayhawks, 20-0. K-State had 270 yards rushing, KU just 47. Kent Duwe carried the ball 33 times for 140 yards to lead the Wildcats' attack.

November 30 - Eighth-ranked Nebraska struggles a little, but prevails in the end over K-State, 20-0. The Wildcats come home with a final record of 2-7.

1941

September 27 - Fort Hays State surprises the Wildcats and fights to a 0-0 tie.

November 8 - K-State defeats South Carolina, 3-0.

November 15 - KU defeats the Wildcats in Lawrence, 20-16.

November 22 - Mike Zeleznak gains 117 yards as K-State ties Iowa State, 12-12.

December 1 - K-State surprises Nebraska at Homecoming and wins, 12-6. Zeleznak gains 133 yards rushing in the win. The Wildcats finish the season with a record of 2-5-2. Adams ends his first tour of duty as K-State's coach with an overall record of 4-12-2.

1942

Ward Haylett is K-State's new football coach.

September 19 - K-State gains an easy win over Kansas Wesleyan, 37-6.

October 24 - Kansas defeats K-State, 19-7.

November 3 - Wichita shuts out the Wildcats, 9-0.

November 21 - The Wildcats squeak out a win over Iowa State, 7-6.

November 28 - K-State surprises Nebraska again, this time defeating the Cornhuskers 19-0 in Lincoln. K-State closes the season with a record of 3-8.

Ward Haylett

1943

October 2 - Washburn falls to K-State in Manhattan, 13-7.

November 6 - Nebraska ruins Homecoming and defeats the Wildcats, 13-7.

November 20 - Iowa State clobbers K-State in Ames, 48-0. K-State is 1-7 for the season.

1944

September 30 - Wichita and K-State fight to a 6-6 tie.

November 4 - K-State travels to Wichita and this time defeats the Wheatshockers, 15-0.

November 11 - A little luck prevailed for the Wildcats as they defeated Kansas on Homecoming weekend, 18-14. KU's quarterback Charles Moffett faked a pass with 15 seconds remaining in the game, made a couple of cut-backs and raced 80 yards for what appeared to be a game-winning touchdown for Kansas. But a clipping penalty at the K-State 20-yard-line called back the run, and the game was over.

November 25 - Nebraska easily defeats the Wildcats, 35-0. K-State goes 2-5-2 for the year. Ward Haylett finishes his time as K-State coach with a 6-20-2 record.

1945

Lud Fiser takes over the head football coach's job at K-State.

September 29 - K-State defeats Wichita in Manhattan for its only victory of the season, 13-6.

November 10 - K-State loses to Nebraska on Homecoming weekend, 24-0.

November 17 - Kansas shuts out the Wildcats, 27-0. Fiser ends his one-year stint at K-State with a 1-7 record.

1946

Hobbs Adams returns to coach the Wildcats again.

September 28 - Hardin-Simmons defeats the Wildcats, 21-7.

November 16 - Kansas rolls over the Wildcats in Manhattan, winning 34-0.

November 30 - Arizona defeats K-State in the season finale, 28-7. Hobbs Adams' one season return ends as the Wildcats finish with an 0-9 record, as well as owning a 16-game losing streak.

1947

Sam Francis is selected to coach K-State.

September 20 - The Wildcats play under the lights at Memorial Stadium for the first time. Oklahoma A&M spoils the evening and wins, 12-0.

K-State punts against KU in 1947.

October 25 - A crowd of 17,000 Homecoming fans watched in disbelief for most of the game as K-State flirted with upsetting Nebraska. The Cornhuskers prevailed in the end, 14-7, but it took two fourth-quarter touchdowns for Nebraska to claim the win.

November 1 - No mercy from KU. K-State takes a terrible pounding from the Jayhawks in Lawrence, losing 55-0.

> *Whatever the psychological elements were, the lowly Wildcats were fired up. Maybe it was partly because of a remark by General Dwight Eisenhower, honored guest at the game, this morning.*
>
> *The general urged the Wildcats to go in and "rock 'em and sock 'em." And that's just what the inspired crew did.*
>
> - From *The Kansas City Star's* K-State-Nebraska game account, October 26, 1947

November 29 - K-State loses to Florida, 25-7, and for the second season in a row finish the football campaign winless with an 0-10 record. The team also holds a 26-game losing streak. Sam Francis ends his one-year stint as the K-State coach.

1948

K-State hires Ralph Graham, one of the school's greatest players, to coach the football team. Graham came to Manhattan after coaching Wichita.

October 2 - Iowa State extends the Wildcats' losing streak to 28, defeating them 20-0.

October 9 - K-State ends its 28-game losing streak, handily defeating Arkansas State in Manhattan, 37-6. It is the Wildcats only win of the season.

October 30 - The eighth-ranked Missouri Tigers down K-State at Homecoming, 49-7.

November 25 - Washington (St. Louis) beats K-State, 21-7. The Wildcats finish the year with a 1-9 record.

1949

Center Harold Robinson became the first African-American to play football at K-State in 1949, and was the first of his race to be named All-Conference in the Big Seven.

September 24 - The Wildcats thrash Fort Hays State, 55-0.

A K-State back struggles for yardage against KU in 1949.

October 15 - Gerald Hackney rips through the Iowa State defense for 162 yards, but the Cyclones still prevail in Ames, 25-21.

Gerald Hackney slashes through would-be tacklers in action from 1950.

November 5 - The third-ranked Oklahoma Sooners shut out K-State, 39-0.

November 24 - Missouri stops K-State in Columbia, 34-27. K-State ends the season with a 2-8 record.

1950

September 16 - Baker is humiliated by the Wildcats, 55-0.

November 4 - K-State loses its Homecoming game to Iowa State, 13-7.

November 11 - Nebraska has an easy time with the Wildcats, 49-21.

December 2 - K-State and Wichita fight to a 6-6 tie in the season finale. K-State finishes with a 1-9-1 record. Ralph Graham's final record as K-State's coach is 4-26-1.

1951

Bill Meek is hired to coach K-State.

October 6 - Swimming in a sea of mud, K-State and Nebraska played to a 6-6 tie in Manhattan. The Wildcats dominated the game statistically, but couldn't score more than one touchdown. Both teams missed their extra-point attempts. K-State ran up 204 rushing yards on the sloppy field. Note: K-State was later ordered to forfeit this game to Nebraska, 1-0.

October 13 - Iowa State defeats K-State, 32-6. The lone Wildcats' touchdown came on Eldon Zellers' 89-yard kickoff return.

November 10 - Tulsa subdues K-State, 42-26.

November 17 - K-State defeated Missouri for the first time in Columbia since 1933, picking off seven passes in the 14-12 victory. K-State also punted 12 times in the game. Note: The Wildcats were later forced to forfeit this game to Missouri, 1-0. The Wildcats officially finish the year at 0-9 (their mark without the forfeits is 1-7-1). Because of the forfeited games, K-State's winless streak is extended to 19 games.

1952

September 20 - Bradley falls to K-State in Manhattan, 21-7, ending the 19-game losing streak.

October 25 - Oklahoma, ranked No. 3 in the country, toys with the Wildcats, 49-6.

November 1 - The ninth-ranked Jayhawks face a game K-State team, but prevail in Lawrence, 26-6.

November 22 - Iowa State defeats K-State 27-0. The Wildcats finish with a 1-9 record.

1953

September 19 - K-State crushes Drake, 50-0.

October 3 - The Wildcats shut out Nebraska, 27-0.

October 17 - K-State stops the Buffaloes in Manhattan, 28-14. Corky Taylor has a great day, gaining 177 yards on the ground in the win.

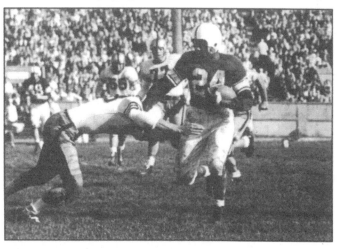

Veryl Switzer eludes another opponent.

November 7 - The Jayhawks found it almost impossible to stop Veryl Switzer, and when the game was over, he had fashioned a 167-yard rushing performance and K-State had a 7-0 win. The game also marked the first time a K-State game was broadcast on network TV (NBC).

November 21 - Using a couple of fumble recoveries to spark a rally, K-State came from behind to tie Arizona, 26-26. Veryl Switzer had a spectacular day, scoring on a 54-yard touchdown pass and returning a punt 81 yards for another score. The tie put K-State's record for the season at 6-3-1.

1954

September 18 - Colorado State falls to the Wildcats in Manhattan, 29-0.

September 25 - The Wildcats defeat Wyoming on the road, 21-13. Corky Taylor runs for 188 yards and Gene Keady adds another 132 to lead the K-State offense.

October 9 - Nebraska falls to K-State for the second year in a row, 7-3.

October 30 - Kansas State beats up on the Jayhawks, winning 28-6 in Manhattan.

November 20 - With a trip to the Orange Bowl on the line, K-State traveled to Boulder, Colorado, to earn the bowl bid, but fell far short in its efforts and lost to the Buffaloes, 38-14. Colorado's offense ran all over K-State, racking up 493 rushing yards. The loss ended the Wildcats' season and left them with a 7-3 record. Bill Meek leaves K-State to become the head coach at the University of Houston.

1955

Bus Mertes takes over as K-State's head football coach.

October 8 - The Wildcats dominate Marquette, 41-0, for their first win of the season. K-State's record is 1-3 after the win.

October 29 - The top-ranked Oklahoma Sooners defeat the Wildcats at Homecoming, 40-7.

The 1955 Kansas State Wildcats

November 5 - The Jayhawks are plucked. K-State scored two touchdowns in the first five minutes of the game and rolled to an easy 46-0 win over KU. The Wildcats gained 298 yards rushing, another 43 through the air, and by halftime led, 33-0. K-State halfback Keith Wilson led the scoring barrage with two tallies. Doug Roether, Ken Nesmith and Bill Carrington crossed the goal once. The Wildcats' defense picked off four passes, with Dick Allen returning one 55 yards for a touchdown. It's the first time since 1924-27 the Wildcats have defeated KU three years in a row.

November 19 - Oklahoma State defeats the Wildcats in the last game of the season, 28-0. K-State finishes with a record of 4-6.

KU defenders (dark jerseys) spent most of the 1955 K-State game chasing Wildcat runners.

1956

October 13 - K-State knocks off the Cornhuskers in Lincoln, 10-7, the Cats' first win of the season.

November 3 - K-State loses to KU for the first in four years, 20-15.

November 10 - K-State smothers Marquette and wins easily, 41-14. Gene Keady runs for 113 yards in the win.

November 17 - The Wildcats have an easy time at Homecoming, defeating Iowa State, 32-6.

November 24 - The 10th-ranked Michigan State Spartans knock off K-State in the season's final game, 38-17. K-State's record for the year is 3-7.

Gene Keady was K-State's top scorer in 1956 with 43 points. Keady has gone on to establish himself as one of the nation's top basketball coaches at Purdue University.

1957

September 28 - Kansas State has an easy time against BYU and defeats the Cougars, 36-7.

October 19 - Homecoming brings another loss as Colorado beats K-State, 42-14.

November 2 - The Oklahoma Sooners' No. 2 ranking doesn't mean much to K-State, but the Wildcats can't pull off the upset and lose, 13-0.

November 16 - Behind the running of Ralph Pfeifer, K-State knocks off Missouri in Columbia, 23-21. Pfeifer gained 106 yards on the ground in the game.

November 23 - Top-ranked Michigan State gets a little more than it expected, but still knocks off K-State, 27-9. The Wildcats finish the '57 season at 3-6-1.

The Kansas State Marching Band at Memorial Stadium.

1958

September 20 - The Wildcats open the season in Manhattan with a 17-14 win over Wyoming.

October 11 - Nebraska falls to K-State in Lincoln, 23-6.

October 18 - Another Homecoming loss, this time to Mizzou. The Tigers stymie the Wildcats, 32-8.

November 15 - K-State drops the Cyclones, defeating Iowa State, 14-6.

November 22 - Michigan State hands the Wildcats a loss in the season finale, 26-7, and K-State finishes with a 3-7 mark for the year.

1959

The school officially changes its name to Kansas State University.

September 19 - Wichita comes to Manhattan and shuts out the Wildcats, 19-0.

September 26 - KSU drops South Dakota State, 28-12.

November 21 - K-State finishes the season on a winning note, beating Nebraska at home, 29-14. KSU posts a 2-8 record for the year. Bus Mertes resigns after the season.

1960

Doug Weaver replaces Mertes as K-State's next head coach.

Doug Weaver

September 17 - The Wildcats sweat out a win against South Dakota State, 20-6. Playing in 90-degree weather in Manhattan, KSU didn't put the game away until Bill Gallagher rambled 81 yards for a touchdown in the fourth quarter. Gallagher finished the day with 117 yards.

October 8 - K-State loses to Nebraska, 17-7.

October 29 - The sixth-ranked Minnesota Golden Gophers easily defeat K-State, 48-7.

November 19 - Arizona defeats the Wildcats, 35-16. Kansas State ends the season with 1-9 record.

1961

September 23 - KSU stops Indiana in the season opener, 14-8.

September 30 - Another win. Air Force is grounded by the Wildcats, 14-12.

November 4 - KSU plays the Oklahoma Sooners tough in Manhattan, losing 17-6.

November 25 - Oklahoma State shuts out the Wildcats, 45-0. The season ends with KSU at 2-8.

1962

September 22 - Indiana stops the Wildcats, 21-0.

October 6 - Playing in its third straight road game to start the season, K-State is dominated by No. 8 Washington, 41-0.

October 20 - Nebraska allows what no other team had this season; K-State finally scores some points after being shut out in the first four games of the season. The Cornhuskers still win, 26-6.

November 10 - The Wildcats lose a heartbreaker at Arizona, 14-13. Willis Crenshaw stars for KSU in the game, running for 102 yards.

November 24 - Oklahoma State ends KSU's season by defeating them in Manhattan, 30-6. It is a horrible year for the Wildcats, who were shut out in six games. They finish at 0-10.

1963

September 21 - BYU visits Manhattan and returns to Utah with a loss. K-State defeats the Cougars, 24-7.

October 26 - No. 7 Oklahoma wins K-State's annual Homecoming game, 34-9.

November 16 - For the first time since 1959, K-State collected a win against a Big Eight opponent as it defeated Iowa State in Ames, 21-10. "We just joined the conference," K-State's elated coach Doug Weaver said after the game. Two fourth-quarter touchdowns lead the way in the win. The Wildcats ran for 218 yards in the game, and passed just seven times.

> "It is the greatest athletic thrill of my career. And what makes it even better, we beat a real outstanding team."
> - K-State coach Doug weaver following the Cats' 21-10 win over Iowa State in 1963

November 23 - K-State's game with Oklahoma State is canceled because of the assassination of President Kennedy. It is not rescheduled, and the Wildcats end the season with a 2-7 record.

1964

October 3 - KSU defeats Colorado, 16-14, in Boulder.

October 31 - Homecoming against the Jayhawks, but the Wildcats can't find their Halloween tricks and lose a close one, 7-0.

November 21 - K-State shoots down Oklahoma State, defeating the Cowboys in Manhattan, 17-14.

November 28 - New Mexico drops the Wildcats in the season finale, 9-7. KSU goes 3-7 for the year.

1965

September 19 - Indiana defeats the Wildcats, 19-7.

October 30 - The Jayhawks blank the Wildcats in Lawrence, 34-0.

November 20 - Oklahoma State finishes off the Wildcats for the season, defeating them 31-7 in Stillwater. KSU finishes with a dismal 0-10 record.

1966

September 17 - Army stops the Cats at West Point, 21-6. Cornelius Davis has a big game for K-State in the loss, gaining 161 yards on the ground.

October 15 - Dave Jones catches eight passes for 188 yards as the Wildcats play Nebraska close, but lose, 21-10.

October 22 - Kansas State can't stop Cincinnati and lose 28-14. Cornelius Davis had another big game for the Wildcats, rushing for 172 yards.

Dave Jones

October 29 - A late fumble by K-State quarterback Bill Nossek gave KU the break it needed, and with eight seconds left in the game, the Jayhawks' Thermus Butler booted a 38-yard field goal to tie the game, 3-3. "It's obvious to everyone that they (his K-State players) played their hearts out," K-State coach Doug Weaver said afterwards. "I'm proud of my team."

> *"If it doesn't show on me, I can't tell you, I suppose I've felt worse, but I don't remember when."*
> - K-State coach Doug Weaver after KU kicked a last-second field goal to tie KSU, 3-3, in 1966

November 19 - K-State closes out the season with a 21-6 loss to Oklahoma State and finish the year with a record of 0-9-1. This game also marked the end of Doug Weaver's coaching career at KSU; his overall record was 8-60-1 in seven seasons.

1967

Vince Gibson is hired as K-State's new football coach.

September 23 - The "Purple Pride" era begins with a 17-7 win over Colorado State. The win ends a 21-game winless streak for the Cats.

October 7 - The Wildcats come close, but fall to No. 7 Nebraska in Manhattan, 16-14.

October 21 - Oklahoma spoils Wildcats' Homecoming, 46-7.

Vince Gibson

November 4 - Close, but still a loss. K-State come within one point of the Jayhawks, but lose in Lawrence, 17-16.

November 11 - Danny Lankas makes a team-record 28 tackles against Missouri, but KSU can't hold back the Tigers and lose, 28-6.

November 25 - The Wildcats take a pounding from Oklahoma State, 49-14. Gibson ends his first year at KSU with a record of 1-9.

1968

K-State played the first game in KSU Stadium on September 21, 1968.

September 21 - The Wildcats open play in KSU Stadium, and win in style over Colorado State, 21-0.

October 5 - The Wildcats handle Virginia Tech, winning 34-19. Mack Herron returns a kickoff 99 yards for a touchdown in the game.

November 2 - Herron returns a kickoff a school-record 100 yards for a touchdown against the Sooners, but Oklahoma prevails in the game, 35-20.

November 9 - The gloomy cold in Nebraska's Memorial Stadium embraced Kansas State as it out-fought and out-played the Cornhuskers to capture a 12-0 win. The victory snapped a four-year drought of conference wins for KSU. "These kids haven't known many victories," Vince Gibson said after the game. "That's what makes a big one like this taste just a little sweeter." Lynn Dickey passed for 217 yards and hit Mack Herron on a nine-yard scoring strike in the first quarter. Max Arreguin booted two field goals in the fourth quarter to seal the win. His second field goal was from 50 yards, the longest kick in K-State history. The Wildcats' defense was super throughout the game, holding Nebraska to 146 yards of total offense and allowing the Big Red to enter purple territory only three times the entire game.

> *"I'm so proud of those kids it's hard to come up with the proper words. They've worked so hard, given it their best every time. It's tough on them to keep getting beat and not have many rewards to show for it."*
> - K-State coach Vince Gibson following the Wildcats' 12-0 win over Nebraska in 1968

November 16 - Homecoming at KSU, and once again KU invades Manhattan. K-State plays the seventh-ranked Jayhawks tight throughout the game, but finally fall, 38-29.

Mack Herron outruns two Virginia Tech defenders to score on a 77-yard run in 1968. KSU won the game, 34-19.

November 23 - KSU finishes a good rebuilding year by defeating Oklahoma State in Manhattan, 21-14. The Wildcats post a 4-6 record for the season.

1969

September 20 - The Wildcats travel to Texas and put a whipping on Baylor, 48-15. Mack Herron stars for KSU, gaining 123 yards on the ground.

October 11 - Fourteen years of frustration were wiped away at KU's Memorial Stadium as K-State out-dueled the Jayhawks and beat its top rival, 26-22. Lynn Dickey had another great day passing, and led the Wildcats on

Vince Gibson and Lynn Dickey discuss strategy.

scoring drives of 80, 90 and 62 yards. Mack Herron scored three touchdowns and KSU receiver Sonny Yarnell made two critical catches. But the biggest play for K-State came on the game's final play when Wildcat defensive backs Clarence Scott and Mike Kolich jarred the ball loose from KU's Steve Conley in the end zone. "I ain't never lived through one like that,"

Lynn Dickey flips a screen pass to Mike Montgomery in the 1969 game against KU.

Vince Gibson said after the game. "We wanted it so bad; we needed it for our program." K-State fans tore down the goalposts following the game. More than 51,000 fans attended the game.

October 18 - Max Arreguin boots a 53-yard field goal, a new school record, in the Wildcats' 34-7 win over Iowa State.

October 25 - Sporting a new No. 18 ranking in the national polls, K-State treated its Homecoming crowd to one of the school's most magnificent, lopsided wins ever. Oklahoma, ranked 11th, caught a dose of Purple Pride and from the second quarter on, there was no doubt about who would win the game. K-State triumphed, 59-21. Lynn Dickey threw for 380 yards and three touchdowns in the Sooner slaughter, and KSU added another 155 yards on the ground. Mack Herron scored three touchdowns, and the Wildcats' defense chipped in with four turnovers. "Before the game we told our kids we were gonna win, and that we had a better football team," K-State coach Vince Gibson said after the game.

November 1 - Sitting on a 5-1 record and a No. 12 national ranking, K-State stormed into Columbia, Missouri, to take on the Tigers in one of the school's biggest games to date. Mizzou, the 14th-ranked team in the country, was up for the task and the teams battled in classic fashion. Trailing 20-6 at the half, Dickey led the Cats back and at one point KSU led, 31-30. "It was a case of whoever had the ball last would win," Dickey said of the game, "which they did." Mizzou got the win in the end, 41-38.

November 8 - KSU loses to Oklahoma State, 28-19. Lynn Dickey has a good game in the defeat, passing for 394 yards. The loss drops the Wildcats out of the Top 20.

November 15 - Nebraska drops the Wildcats in Manhattan, 10-7.

November 22 - Lynn Dickey throws for 439 yards, a school record at the time, and Mack Herron pulls in 12 passes for 171 yards, but the Wildcats lose to Colorado, 45-32. KSU has its best season since 1954 and finishes with a 5-5 record.

1970

September 12 - K-State blanks Utah State, 37-0, to start the season.

October 3 - The Wildcats win a thriller from the eighth-ranked Colorado Buffaloes, 21-20.

October 7 - The Big Eight Conference places K-State on probation for recruiting violations, and rocks the school with some of the stiffest penalties ever. The Wildcats are barred from post-season play and any television appearances for three years (through the end of the 1972 season).

> "Lynn is the link in our chain. Without him, the link is only temporary. He's a super player, but it's more than his physical ability; it's what he does to our confidence that's the real thing. You just know he's going to do his job."
> - KSU fullback Mike Montgomery, 1970

October 10 - Kansas State ran up and down the field against the Jayhawks, racking up 249 yards passing and 138 yards rushing, but a fumbled punt snap and an illegal procedure penalty gave KU a touchdown and took one away from K-State. In the end, the outgunned Jayhawks prevailed, 21-15. "There might be some sick people," K-State coach Vince Gibson bemoaned after the game, "but they got their money's worth ... I think we've got a better football team, but we didn't win the game."

Lynn Dickey

October 24 - K-State knocks off the Sooners for the second straight year, 19-14. Dickey passes for 384 yards in the win.

October 31 - Lynn Dickey marched the Wildcats 70 yards in the final four minutes to lead Kansas State to a dramatic win over Missouri, 17-13. Dickey hit Mike Creed from 20 yards out for the game-winning score. "This might be the biggest win since I've been here," a happy Vince Gibson said after the game. Dickey shook off four first-half interceptions and finished the game with 234 yards passing. Creed had 126 receiving yards on five receptions in the victory.

Mike Montgomery flies for yardage in 1970 action.

The 1970 Kansas State Wildcats

November 7 - Bill Butler runs for 130 yards as KSU drops Oklahoma State, 28-15.

November 14 - With a bowl game an impossibility because of the NCAA probation, K-State goes to Nebraska as the 20th-ranked team in the country, and determined to capture the Big Eight crown. The Cornhuskers have other ideas, though, and the Wildcats suffer an embarrassing defeat, 51-13.

November 22 - Florida State defeats K-State, 31-7, in the season's final game. The loss puts the Wildcats record for the season at 6-5.

1971

September 18 - KSU travels to Tulsa and stops the Golden Hurricane, 19-10.

September 25 - Bill Butler rushes for 142 yards in the Wildcats' 23-7 win over BYU.

October 16 - Iowa State defeats Kansas State at Homecoming, 24-0.

October 23 - The No. 2 ranked OU Sooners roll past K-State in Manhattan, 75-28.

October 30 - Kansas State defeats Missouri, 28-12. Henry Childs catches six passes for 144 yards in the win.

November 20 - The Wildcats drop Memphis State, 28-21, and conclude the season with a 5-6 record.

1972

Don Calhoun

September 9 - The Wildcats defeat Tulsa in Manhattan, 21-13.

September 16 - Don Calhoun gains 132 yards on the ground, but BYU stifles the rest of the Cats and wins, 32-9.

October 14 - Playing more against a 30-mile-an-hour wind than the Jayhawks, K-State jumped to an early 14-0 lead and then held on to defeat Kansas, 20-19. Reserve cornerback Jim Cunningham made the play of the game for K-State, slamming KU quarterback David Jaynes out of bounds at the one-yard-line on a two-point conversion attempt that would have given the Jayhawks the lead. KSU quarterback Dennis Morrison threw just eight times, but two of the passes were for touchdowns. Isaac Jackson had a big game running the ball, netting 110 yards. "Those kids (K-State players) have had such a tough year," Vince Gibson said after the game. "And the seniors had never beaten KU. That victory lap after the game was their idea. This KU and K-State rivalry is super for the state."

November 18 - Nebraska has an easy time with K-State, 59-7. The Wildcats finish the season with a record of 3-8.

1973

September 22 - The Wildcats shut down Tulsa and win, 21-0. Isaac Jackson gains 157 yards on the ground to lead the offense.

October 6 - The Wildcats wind up their rushing offense and ground out a win over Memphis State, 21-16. Isaac Jackson gains 131 yards rushing and Steve Grogan adds another 100 yards in the win.

October 13 - K-State fights the 19th-ranked Jayhawks to the end of the game, but lose on a late touchdown by KU quarterback David Jaynes, 25-18.

October 20 - KSU ekes out a win over Iowa State in Manhattan, 21-19.

October 27 - The third-ranked OU Sooners boom the Wildcats on Homecoming, 56-14.

November 24 - Kansas State drops the Buffaloes in Boulder, 17-14. The win improves the Cats' final record for the year to 5-6.

1974

September 14 - K-State drops Tulsa to start the season with a 31-14 win in Manhattan.

September 21 - Roscoe Scobey rips through the Shockers for 155 yards rushing, and K-State defeats Wichita State, 17-0.

Steve Grogan

October 12 - For second year in a row the Jayhawks come back and defeat K-State, 20-13. A malfunctioning clock forced time to be kept on the field, and the confusion cost K-State in the waning seconds of the game. K-State quarterback Steve Grogan was stopped two yards short of the goal-line on the game's final play.

November 23 - The Vince Gibson era ends with a stunning 33-19 win over Colorado. Steve Grogan threw for 120 yards and a score, and fullback James Couch ran the ball into the end zone twice. The win put K-State at 4-7 for the season. Gibson, who had revitalized K-State football with his "Purple Pride" slogan, left the school with an overall record of 33-52.

> *"I told 'em (the football team) this could be the last game for the coaching staff. I said I wanted the seniors to leave with their heads up. I wanted a win for our young kids to come back, believin' they can win."*
> - Vince Gibson, after K-State defeated Colorado 33-19 in 1974

1975

Ellis Rainsberger is named as K-State's new football coach.

September 13 - Led by its defense's three game-saving stands in the final six minutes of the game, K-State held on and defeated Tulsa, 17-16. Ellis Rainsberger, the Wildcats' new head coach, got the win in his first game as the school's top man. K-State picked up 211 yards on the ground. "I just thought our team fought their hearts out from the opening kickoff," Rainsberger said afterwards. "Was I shaky? I was a little shaky at the end. Well, I was shaky at the start and in the middle, too."

September 20 - The Wildcats shut out Wichita State in Manhattan, 32-0.

September 27 - K-State has another close game and defeats Wake Forest, 17-16. Roscoe Scobey gains 105 yards on the ground to lead the offense.

October 4 - The sixth-ranked Texas A&M Aggies get more of a game than they expected in Manhattan, but prevail over KSU, 10-0.

November 8 - No. 3 Nebraska struggles against the Cats in Manhattan before winning, 12-0.

November 22 - Colorado defeats K-State in Boulder, 33-7. KSU ends with a 3-8 record for the year.

1976

September 11 - Brigham Young comes to Manhattan and goes home losers. K-State defeats the Cougars, 13-3. Bill Sinovic boots a school record 58-yard field goal in the game.

October 9 - K-State plays on par with the Missouri Tigers throughout the game, but lose, 28-21.

October 23 - The Jayhawks prove too much to handle and beat the Wildcats in Manhattan, 24-14.

November 20 - The 15th-ranked Colorado Buffaloes claim a win over the Wildcats in the season finale, 35-28. KSU posts a 1-10 record for the year.

1977

September 10 - BYU exacts a little revenge for losses from earlier seasons and beats the Wildcats in Utah, 39-0.

September 24 - K-State travels to Wichita and defeats the Wheatshockers, 21-14.

October 1 - Mississippi State defeats K-State, 24-21. KSU running back Mack Green has a field day against the Bulldogs in the loss, and rushes for 181 yards. The game is later forfeited to the Wildcats.

November 5 - Kansas uses a long touchdown run by halfback Max Ediger to subdue the Wildcats in Lawrence. KU wins, 29-21.

November 19 - Colorado ends K-State's season with a loss, 23-0. KSU goes 1-10 for the season (2-9 after the forfeit). This was also Ellis Rainsberger's final game as K-State's coach. He compiled an overall record of 6-27 in three seasons.

1978

Jim Dickey takes over as the new head football coach at K-State.

September 9 - Arizona spoils Jim Dickey's debut and easily disposes of K-State, 31-0. "We got beat by a better team," Dickey said after the game.

> *"The Wildcats haven't won a conference championship in 40 years. Well, if I don't win a championship in that same length of time, I'll resign."*
> *- Jim Dickey*

September 30 - Mack Green rushes for 123 yards as the Wildcats earn their first victory of the season and defeat Air Force, 34-21. K-State amassed 450 yards of offense in the game.

October 7 - The Wildcats down Oklahoma State, 18-7. Roosevelt Duncan runs for 126 yards against the Cowboys.

> "We made it understood as a team and to ourselves that we weren't going to lose this game. Now we've got the conference season, and we're going to win some-we can beat some of the teams in the Big Eight."
> - KSU quarterback Dan Manucci after the Wildcats defeated Air Force in 1978

Jim Dickey

November 11 - K-State pulls off a big win against Colorado, 20-10. L. J. Brown rips off 138 yards rushing against the Buffaloes.

November 18 - Jayhawk stew. Kansas State raced to 30-0 lead and eventually defeated KU at home, 36-20. "Everything went right today," KSU's Tony Brown said of the game. "Everyone had confidence in each other. We've had some hard times this season, but it all came together at the end." The win set the Wildcats' final record at 4-7.

A Wildcat runner pounds out yardage against KU in 1978.

1979

September 22 - The Wildcats down Oregon State in Manhattan, 22-16.

September 29 - L. J. Brown has a tremendous running day and gains 200 yards rushing, and Roosevelt Duncan adds another 100 yards on the ground as K-State defeats Air Force, 19-6.

October 27 - K-State shocks Missouri in Columbia, 19-3. The Wildcats' freshman quarterback, Darrell Dickey, passed for 187 yards and two touchdowns to lead KSU. "I'm extremely happy for the players," K-State coach Jim Dickey said afterwards. "They lost some close games before today and could have thrown in the towel for the rest of the season."

November 10 - KSU scares No. 2 Nebraska, but the Cornhuskers still win in Manhattan, 21-12.

November 24 - KSU loses to Colorado, 21-6, and ends the year with a 3-8 mark.

1980

September 20 - K-State drops South Dakota for its first win of the season, 24-3.

November 1 - Trailing 20-10 with 2:30 left in the game, K-State blocked a KU punt and scored on the next play. A two-point conversion pulled the Cats within two points, but the Jayhawks recovered the onside kick and were able to run out the clock to win, 20-18. Kansas was later ordered to forfeit the game because of recruiting violations.

November 22 - L. J. Brown rushes for 148 yards and the Wildcats close out the season with a 17-14 win over Colorado at home. KSU goes 4-7 for the year.

1981

K-State coach Jim Dickey decides to redshirt the returning seniors for the 1981 season, hoping the extra year of maturity will propel the Wildcats to a higher level of play in the 1982 season.

September 12 - K-State gets an easy win over South Dakota to open the season, 31-10. Wildcat quarterback Darrell Dickey runs for 126 yards in the game.

October 31 - The Cats squeeze by Iowa State, 10-7.

November 7 - Kansas State makes a strong bid for a major upset before falling to Oklahoma, 28-21. The Wildcats jumped to a 21-0 lead, their first touchdown coming on a 20-play, 80-yard drive in the first quarter. Mark Hundley scored the Cats' first touchdown. The Sooners scored the winning touchdown with 2:36 left in the game.

November 21 - K-State falls short against Colorado and loses in Boulder, 24-21. KSU records a 2-9 record for the season.

1982

Darrell Dickey

September 11 - Stacked with its group of fifth-year seniors, K-State starts the season with a 23-9 win over Kentucky at KSU Stadium.

September 25 - Wichita State falls to the Wildcats in Manhattan, 31-7. The newly created Wheat State Trophy would eventually belong to K-State.

October 9 - KSU and Mizzou finish in a 7-7 tie.

October 23 - A crowd of 45,595 jammed into KSU Stadium under portable lights to witness the Wildcats total dismantling of the Jayhawks. Sporting special gray uniforms for the game, K-State dominated from start to finish and wiped out KU, 36-7. The game was televised nationally on superstation WTBS.

November 13 - Mike Wallace catches seven passes for 146 yards, but the Wildcats fail to lock up a bowl bid and fall to Oklahoma State, 24-16.

November 20 - After 87 years of waiting, K-State received its first-ever bowl berth after defeating Colorado, 33-10, at KSU Stadium. KSU's impatient fans dismantled the goalposts before the game officially ended, but it didn't matter to Coach Jim Dickey. "I forgive every one of them, they have been waiting for so long," he said after the

> *"A number of people asked me throughout the year how I thought the redshirt program would work. It looks pretty good now. Leadership is one good reason. The seniors gave us a lot of it this season ... they were tremendous."*
>
> - Jim Dickey, following K-State's bowl-clinching win over Colorado in 1982

game. The Wildcats' offense had a potent running game, as Iosefatu Faraimo and Masi Toluao both ran for 97 yards. Faraimo also scored twice. Fullback Mike Pierson rumbled 55 yards for the Cats' final, clinching touchdown late in the game.

December 11 - Bad night in Shreveport. Kansas State faces Wisconsin in the Independence Bowl, the school's first-ever bowl game. Fighting the bad weather as well as the Badgers, the Wildcats were unable to sustain any kind of offensive threat in the game and lose, 14-3. But the season is still a success, and the Wildcats finish with a 6-5-1 record, the team's best showing since 1970.

Kansas State safety Jim Bob Morris is ready for the Wildcats' trip to the Independence Bowl.

Action from K-State's 36-7 romp over KU in 1982.

1983

September 3 - Kansas State loses to Long Beach State, 28-20.

September 24 - The Wildcats sneak past Wyoming and win at home, 27-25.

November 5 - KSU picks up a road victory, defeating Oklahoma State in Stillwater, 21-20.

November 19 - Colorado defeats K-State, 38-21. The Wildcats finish the season with a 3-8 record.

1984

September 15 - K-State quarterback Stan Weber gains 105 yards rushing in the Wildcats' 28-12 victory against Tennessee Tech in Manhattan.

October 13 - The Wildcats smother the Jayhawks, 24-7.

October 20 - Missouri drubs the Wildcats, 61-21. K-State's Gerald Alphin pulls in three passes for 130 yards.

November 10 - K-State and Iowa State finish in a 7-7 tie.

November 17 - The season ends on a high note as K-State routs the Colorado Buffaloes at KSU Stadium, 38-6. Kent Dean returns an onside kick 47 yards for a touchdown in the game. K-State ends the season with a 3-7-1 record.

1985

Defeat weighed heavily on the Wildcats in 1985.

September 7 - Wichita State drops the Wildcats at KSU Stadium, 16-10.

September 14 - Kansas State suffers a tough loss to Northern Iowa, 10-6. KSU's John Kendrick picks up 142 yards on the ground in the losing effort.

September 15 - Jim Dickey resigns following the Wildcats' loss to Northern Iowa. Lee Moon takes over as the interim head coach.

October 26 - Gerald Alphin catches eight passes for 154 yards against Missouri. K-State edges the Tigers 20-17.

November 23 - Colorado shuts out the Wildcats in the final game of the season, 30-0. The Wildcats finish with a 1-10 record.

1986

Stan Parrish is selected as K-State's new head football coach.

August 30 - K-State knocks off Western Illinois, 35-7.

October 18 - The Wildcats blitz their way to a win over KU, 29-12. KSU sacked Jayhawks quarterback Mike Orth three times, picked off three passes and held him to 13 completions in the game. "We were so pumped up for the game," K-State guard Bob Bessert said

Tony Jordan rips through the Jayhawks.

following the game. " It was a big win, a springboard to push us into the rest of the season." This was the last game K-State would win until 1989.

November 15 - Tony Jordan tears up Iowa State for 218 yards rushing, but the Wildcats are easily defeated by the Cyclones, 48-19.

November 22 - Colorado rips apart the Wildcats, 49-3. K-State finishes with a 2-9 record.

1987

September 5 - Austin Peay State defeats K-State in Manhattan, 26-22.

October 17 - The top-ranked OU Sooners pound K-State, 59-10.

October 24 - The number two ranked Cornhuskers slaughter the Cats, 56-3.

November 7 - Futility never looked so bad. K-State and KU played evenly, but this was a game about not being the worst, and when Mark Porter's 28-yard field goal attempt was blocked with three seconds remaining in the game, both teams left the field losers, even though the final score was 17-17. "The media and people across the country are going to say this ended in appropriate fashion," K-State tight end Kent Dean said afterwards. "But it's not. There should be a winner and loser. To me this is just like losing." Tony Jordan gained 147 yards rushing for KSU, but the turnovers and mistakes in the game, by both teams, over-shadowed his good effort.

November 14 - Trying to rebound from the tie with KU, K-State almost pulls off a mild upset against the Cyclones, but lose, 16-14.

November 21 - Colorado hammers the Wildcats, 41-0. KSU finishes with an 0-10-1 record.

1988

Mark Porter celebrates after kicking a 61-yard field goal against Nebraska in 1988.

September 3 - Tulsa defeats KSU, 35-9.

October 3 - Stan Parrish announces his resignation, effective at the end of the season.

October 15 - The Sooners take no prisoners and dismantle the Wildcats, 70-24.

October 22 - Mark Porter booms a 61-yard field goal for the Wildcats only points against Nebraska. The Cornhuskers won, 48-3. "It was good to get a chance to do a long one like that because everyone asks you what your longest field goal is," Porter said. "Mostly, though I was just happy Coach Parrish gave me a chance to do it."

October 29 - Lee Pickett runs for 130 yards and Greg Washington catches 11 passes for 157 yards, the Wildcats still fall far short of defeating Oklahoma State, 45-27.

November 5 - Kansas has an easy time against the Wildcats, winning 30-12 in Lawrence.

November 19 - The Wildcats end another winless season in Colorado, losing to the Buffaloes, 56-14. Their record is 0-11 for the year.

November 30 - Bill Snyder is hired to coach the K-State football team.

1989

September 9 - Coach Snyder's debut with the Wildcats is spoiled as Arizona State handily defeats K-State, 31-0.

September 23 - The winless streak reaches 30 games as the Wildcats fall to Northern Illinois in Manhattan, 37-20.

> *"You just don't like to be beaten all the time, within our own professions or our own daily responsibilities. We don't like to be beaten ... 365 bad days year-in and year-out can beat you down, and that's what I saw in these young guys."*
>
> - -Bill Snyder, on the state of his team in 1989

September 30 - It's over! The 30-game streak of winless futility ends as K-State defeats North Texas State, 20-17. With the ball on the North Texas 12-yard line and four seconds remaining in the game, backup quarterback Carl Straw hit Frank Hernandez on a rollout pass, who then tippy-toed into the end zone for the game-winning score. KSU Stadium went berserk. "We'll be cele-

> *"I'm proud of them, I love them, (but) we've got a lot of things to do. One win won't make a total difference. These kids and fans have suffered. I keep telling them this football team is not responsible for 27 of those losses, but I'm not sure they always believed me."*
>
> - Bill Snyder, following the win over North Texas State that ended the Wildcats' 30-game winless streak

brating until 8:30 in the morning, "K-State guard Chad Faulkner said after the game. "On the last play I was blocking a guy, then all of a sudden I heard everybody screaming. It was unreal."

October 7 - Fourth-ranked Nebraska beats up on the Wildcats, 58-7.

October 21 - Michael Smith catches 13 passes for 166 yards, but the Wildcats lose to Missouri, 21-9.

Bill Snyder at the press conference announcing his hiring as K-State's new head football coach.

November 18 - The second-ranked Colorado Buffaloes drop a big score on K-State, winning 59-11. Coach Snyder finishes his first year at KSU with 1-10 mark.

1990

September 15 - Pat Jackson gains 156 yards rushing as the Wildcats destroy New Mexico State, 52-7.

October 13 - Oklahoma State falls to the Wildcats in Manhattan, 23-17.

October 27 - The Jayhawks hang on against the Wildcats in Lawrence and win, 27-24.

November 3 - Iowa State tastes the sting of defeat and fall to K-State at KSU Stadium, 28-14.

November 17 - Colorado walks over the Wildcats in Boulder, 64-3. K-State ends the season with a 5-6 record.

1991

September 7 - Yards by the Gallon. Eric Gallon runs for 184 yards in the Wildcats' 26-25 comeback win over Indiana State.

September 21 - Paul Watson passes for 311 yards as the Wildcats defeat Northern Illinois, 34-17.

Frank Hernandez

Eric Gallon

October 12 - The "Miracle in Manhattan." Overcoming six turnovers, K-State scored two late touchdowns to come-from-behind and sack Kansas, 16-12. A 34-yard touchdown pass from Paul Watson to Andre Coleman gave the Cats the game-winner. The KSU defense then had to stymie a late KU drive to secure the win.

> *"That was probably the ultimate feeling in college football, to come from behind like that and have such a great defensive game as a total defense. To come back and score in the last two minutes, I just remember the family, the friends, the players, everybody was just on an incredible high."*
> — Brooks Barta on K-State's 16-12 win over KU in 1991

November 16 - Eric Gallon chews up the Tigers, ripping through the Mizzou defense for 184 yards. K-State slaps around the Tigers to win going away, 32-0.

November 23 - K-State ends its season by defeating Oklahoma State in Stillwater, 36-26. The Cats finish with a 7-4 record, the team's best mark since 1954.

1992

September 19 - Montana falls to K-State, 27-12.

October 10 - K-State takes a hard loss against the Jayhawks in Lawrence, 31-7. It's the last time the Wildcats have lost to KU.

November 5 - Eric Gallon rips through the Cyclones' defense for 164 yards as K-State downs Iowa State, 22-13, in front of a national ESPN audience.

December 5 - K-State travels to Tokyo to play Nebraska in the Coca-Cola Bowl. The Cornhuskers defeat the Cats, 38-24. KSU finishes with a 5-6 record.

Brooks Barta

1993

September 18 - The Wildcats hold on and defeat Minnesota, 30-25, ending a 14-year non-conference road losing streak. "It was a ballgame of character," Bill Snyder said afterwards. "It was a ballgame of big (plays), and it was a ballgame of special teams." Chad May threw for 247 yards and one touchdown.

October 9 - K-State trips the Jayhawks in Manhattan, 10-9. J. J. Smith runs through the Jayhawks' defense for 135 yards in the win. Chad May hit Andre Coleman for the Wildcats' only touchdown in the game.

J. J. Smith celebrates during the Wildcats' victory over Wyoming in the Copper Bowl.

October 16 - Chad May passes for a school-record 489 yards in the Wildcats' 45-28 loss to Nebraska.

October 30 - Sporting a No. 25 ranking, K-State knocks off the No. 13 Sooners, 21-7. Rod Schiller gains 111 yards rushing in the game.

November 20 - The Wildcats pick up a big win on the road, eclipsing the Oklahoma State Cowboys, 21-17. The Copper Bowl was waiting.

December 29 - Copper Bowl slaughter. The Wildcats take no prisoners and ambush Wyoming, 52-17. It's the first bowl win in the school's history, and it made a strong statement to the rest of the college football world that K-State had arrived as a national power. Chad May threw for 275 yards and two touchdowns, and J. J. Smith picked up 133 yards on the ground. The Wildcats finished the season as the 20th-ranked team in the AP poll with a record of 9-2-1.

> "Kansas State people have proven that they travel well. That certainly will benefit us when we are in a position to have an opportunity to compete in future post-season bowl games."
> - Bill Snyder, after the 1993 Copper Bowl

Chad May

1994

September 24 - The Cats roll over Minnesota, 35-0. J. J. Smith runs for 137 yards against the Gophers.

October 6 - Chad May rips the Jayhawks' defense for 379 yards passing as the Wildcats defeat Kansas, 21-13 on a national ESPN telecast.

October 22 - Chad May passes for 356 yards, but the Wildcats lose to the second-ranked Buffaloes, 35-21.

November 12 - J. J. Smith runs through the Tigers' defense for 138 yards and K-State squeaks by the Missouri Tigers, 21-18.

November 26 - J. J. Smith explodes for 227 yards rushing as the Wildcats have an easy time with UNLV, winning 42-3.

December 25 - It was a bleak Christmas day for K-State as the Boston College Eagles defeated the Wildcats in the Aloha Bowl, 12-7. KSU netted just seven first downs on offense, and had a net of minus-61 yards rushing for the game. Boston College held off a last-chance drive, and walk off the field as the winners. K-state finished with a 9-3 record and a No. 19 ranking in the AP poll.

1995

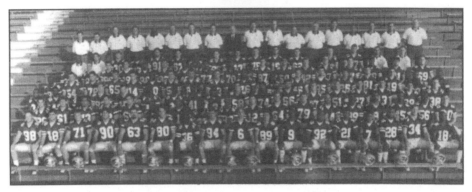

The 1995 Kansas State Wildcats

September 2 - K-State defeats Temple at home, 34-7.

September 9 - K-State quarterback Matt Miller led the Wildcats on a desperation, 59-yard touchdown drive in the final 38 seconds of the game to escape with a victory over Cincinnati, 23-21. Miller hit Kevin Lockett with a 22-yard touchdown pass on the game's final play, and KSU had the win. "It seemed like 10 or 15 seconds passed from the time Matt threw the ball," Lockett said of the game-winning play. "It was like everything was in slow motion." K-State had six turnovers in the game.

October 28 - Proving who really belonged in the Top 10, No. 14 K-State humiliated the sixth-ranked Jayhawks, 41-7, in Manhattan. Using a powerful running attack, K-State was virtually unstoppable the entire game. Eric Hickson and Mike Lawrence both topped the 100-yard rushing mark for the game, as KSU scored early and often in the first half.

November 11 - Eric Hickson rushes for 144 yards as the seventh-ranked Wildcats crush Iowa State, 49-7.

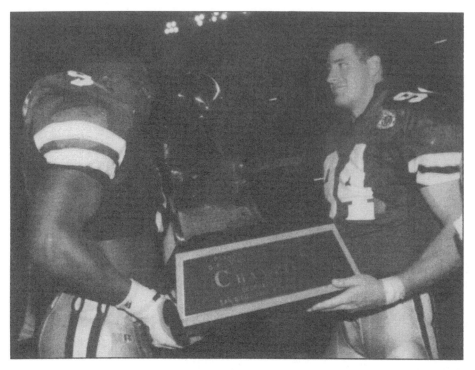

Percell Gaskins and Dirk Ochs with the 1995 Holiday Bowl Trophy.

December 29 - Kansas State routed the Colorado State Rams in the Holiday Bowl, 54-21. Displaying an awesome offense throughout the game, the Wildcats raced to a 26-7 lead at the half. Brian Kavanagh replaced the injured Matt Miller and threw four touchdown passes. The Wildcats finished ranked in the Top 10 for the first time ever, placing seventh in the AP poll. The team's final record was 10-2 for the year.

1996

K-State becomes a part of the new Big 12 Conference.

August 31 - Playing the inaugural Big 12 football game, K-State defeats Texas Tech in Manhattan, 21-14.

October 5 - Nebraska drops the Wildcats in Manhattan, 39-3.

October 12 - Mike Lawrence has a big day, collecting 168 yards on the ground as K-State defeats Missouri in Columbia, 35-10.

October 26 - Brian Kavanagh passes for 349 yards in the Wildcats' 42-35 win over Oklahoma.

November 16 - No. 6 Colorado shuts out the Wildcats in Boulder, 12-0.

November 23 - Mike Lawrence sets the K-State single-game rushing record, gaining 252 yards on the ground in K-State's 35-20 win over Iowa State.

January 1, 1997 - Playing in its first New Year's Day bowl game, Kansas State fell short against the BYU Cougars and lost the Cotton Bowl, 19-15. Brian Kavanagh gained 233 yards in passing, but also threw a couple of costly interceptions. The loss dropped the Wildcats record to 9-3 for the season, and they finished with a No. 17 ranking in both polls.

Chris Canty

1997

September 6 - K-State starts the season on a roll, wiping out Northern Illinois, 47-7.

October 4 - The third-ranked NU Cornhuskers prove to be too much and overwhelm K-State in Lincoln, 56-26.

October 11 - Michael Bishop runs wild, gaining 196 yards on the ground as the Wildcats thump Missouri at home, 41-11.

October 18 - KSU surprises the 14th-ranked Texas A&M Aggies and wins, 36-17. Mike Lawrence rushes for 105 yards in the game.

November 8 - K-State cruises past the Jayhawks, easily winning 48-16. Gerald Neasman returns a kickoff 97 yards for a touchdown in the blowout victory, and David Allen returns a punt 70 yards for another score. Darnell McDonald catches three passes for 106 yards to lead the offense.

November 22 - Mike Lawrence rushes for 102 yards as the ninth-ranked Wildcats defeat Iowa State, 28-3. The win propels KSU into the Fiesta Bowl.

December 31 - Putting a cap on the best season in the school's history, the Wildcats dropped Syracuse in the Fiesta Bowl, 35-18. Michael Bishop passed for 317 yards, and added another 77 on the ground. Darnell McDonald caught seven of Bishop's passes for 206 yards and three touchdowns, including a 77-yarder early in the fourth quarter. The win pushed K-State's final ranking to seventh in the ESPN/USA Today poll, eighth in the AP. The Cats finished with an 11-1 record.

1998

Bill Snyder talks with reporters following K-State's 35-18 victory over Syracuse in the 1997 Fiesta Bowl.

September 12 - Martin Gramatica connects on a 65-yard field goal, the longest in NCAA history without the use of a tee, as the Wildcats run up the second-highest point total in school history and defeat Northern Illinois, 73-7.

September 19 - David Allen returns a punt 93 yards for a touchdown as the Wildcats upend Texas, 48-7.

September 26 - Michael Bishop passes for 441 yards and four touchdowns as the Wildcats clobber Northeast Louisiana, 62-7. Aaron Lockett and Darnell McDonald each have more than 100 yards receiving.

October 10 - Eric Hickson picks up 137 yards on the ground as K-State wins at Colorado, 16-9.

November 7 - K-State whips Baylor, 49-6, and moves into the No. 1 spot in the ESPN/USA Today poll. The Cats are ranked second in the AP poll.

Michael Bishop runs against Nebraska during K-State's 40-30 win in 1998.

November 14 - The happiest place on the planet. K-State defeats Nebraska in a back and forth game, 40-30, and clinches a spot in the Big 12 Championship Game. It was the first time since 1968 the Cats defeated the Huskers. Darnell

> *"I can't think of one that was bigger. I'm happy. I can assure you of that. I feel very good about this win – I am humbled by it."*
> — Bill Snyder, following the 40-30 win over Nebraska in 1998

McDonald caught an 11-yard touchdown pass from Michael Bishop with 5:25 remaining in the game. Jeff Kelly ran 33 yards with a fumble recovery to score the Wildcats' final touchdown with three seconds left in the game. "We have not had to come from behind this year," Coach Snyder said following the game. "I am not sure this team had to come from behind much last year." And he added, "I am so happy and proud for the 10 years of people who laid the groundwork for this."

December 5 - With a shot at the national championship waiting for them if they won, the Wildcats lose a heartbreaking, double-overtime thriller to Texas A&M in the Big 12 Championship Game, 36-33. The loss also ended the Cats' school-record 19-game winning streak. Leading 27-12 going into the fourth quarter, K-State couldn't hold the lead, and gave up 15 points to A&M. The Aggies won in the second OT on 32-yard pass.

December 29 - Kansas State's great season went down in flames as the Wildcats were upset by the unranked Purdue Boilermakers in the Alamo Bowl, 37-34. Trailing most of the game, the Wildcats took the lead with 1:24 remaining, only to see Purdue march the length of the field and score the winning touchdown with 30 seconds left. Michael Bishop threw for 182 yards in the game, but his four interceptions were costly. David Allen was the leading rusher for the Wildcats with 83 yards. K-State finished the season with an 11-2 record and a No. 10 ranking in the AP poll.

1999

September 18 - Frank Murphy gains 156 yards rushing as the Wildcats take care of UTEP in Manhattan, 40-7.

September 25 - David Allen's 94-yard punt return sparked the Wildcats to a great comeback, and they defeated the Iowa State Cyclones in Ames, 35-28.

October 2 - Once again David Allen was the catalyst the Cats needed. His 74-yard punt return midway through the third quarter sent the Wildcats to victory as they defeated Texas, 35-17. It was Allen's seventh punt return for a touchdown in his career.

October 16 - K-State blanks Utah State, 40-0. Joe Hall runs for 195 yards, and Jamie Rheem kicks four field goals, one from 57 yards.

October 23 - Jonathan Beasley passes for 311 yards as the Wildcats come back from a 21-0 deficit to defeat the Oklahoma State Cowboys, 44-21.

November 13 - Nebraska extracted a little revenge for its loss to KSU in 1998 and handily defeated K-State in Lincoln, 41-15. The Wildcats were shut down on offense throughout the game, and outgunned by Nebraska's offensive unit, giving up 309 yards rushing. The Huskers scored 17 points in the final quarter to put the game away.

December 29 - Using a clock-consuming drive and a rugged defense, K-State won a physical contest with Washington to capture the Holiday Bowl. Jonathan Beasley scored three touchdowns to lead the Wildcats, and Quincy Morgan caught eight passes for 104 yards. The defense added five sacks and held the Huskies to 75 yards rushing. The win upped the Cats' record to 11-1, the team's third 11-win season in a row. K-State finished as the sixth-ranked team in both polls.

David Allen turns the corner against Texas in 1999.

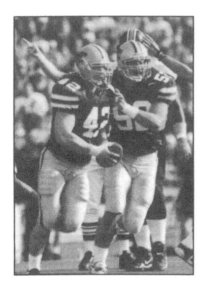

Mark Simoneau and Ben Leber celebrate a turnover against Missouri in 1999.

Bill Snyder accepts the 1999 Holiday Bowl trophy after the Wildcats defeated Washington, 24-20.

The 1999 Kansas State Wildcats

Wildcat
Players Trivia

Michael Bishop

Michael Bishop
1997-98

K-State's greatest quarterback of all-time, Michael Bishop's breathtaking and dazzling style of play led the Wildcats to the 1998 Big 12 Championship game and the school's first-ever No. 1 ranking. A junior college transfer from Texas, Bishop was an exciting scrambler and terrific runner – he broke the school record for most career yards rushing by a quarterback. But it was his passing arm that powered K-State's offense, and his strong, accurate tosses compiled 4,401 yards through the air in his two seasons as the Wildcats' quarterback. Bishop finished his career with a school-record 36 touchdown passes. He put up big numbers throughout his senior season, completing 164 of 295 passes with just four interceptions.

Bishop also left a long list of impressive records and numbers at K-State: a school-record 475 yards of total offense against Northeast Louisiana in 1998, longest pass completion in K-State history, the single-season records for total offense and rushing yardage by a quarterback in 1998, and the K-State career rushing touchdown mark by a quarterback with 23.

A first-team All-American in 1998, Bishop also finished second in the Heisman Trophy voting, a first in the history of K-State football. As the Wildcats' starting quarterback, Bishop led the team to a 22-3 record.

1. What junior college did Bishop attend before coming to K-State?

2. How many games did his junior college team lose while he was the quarterback there?

3. What major college award did Bishop win following his senior season at K-State?

4. How many yards passing did Bishop have in 1998?

5. How many touchdown passes did Bishop throw during the 1998 season?

6. How many touchdowns did Bishop score in 1998?

7. How many yards rushing did he have in 1998?

8. Bishop passed for 441 yards during one game in 1998. Who was the opponent?

9. Bishop finished second in the 1998 Heisman Trophy vote. Who won the Heisman that year?

10. Bishop completed a 97-yard pass for a touchdown in 1998. Who caught the pass, and who was the opponent?

11. What NFL team selected Bishop in the NFL Draft, and in what round was he taken?

Bishop prepares to take a snap against Indiana State in 1998.

Michael Bishop poses with the Davey O'Brien Award after being named the nation's outstanding collegiate quarterback at a banquet in Fort Worth.

Chris Canty

Chris Canty

1994-96

Throughout his three years in Kansas State's defensive backfield, Chris Canty was nothing less than sensational.

"He just had an excellent game," Bob Stoops said, who was K-State's defensive coordinator during Canty's career. "What makes him so good is the fact that he has great ball skills. He has a knack for playing the football, catching it and judging it. He just has a good feel for the game."

A prep All-American in high school at Voorhees, New Jersey, Canty's three-year run in K-State's defensive backfield was outstanding. He had 169 total tackles, became the No. 2 all-time interception leader at the school, was a unanimous first-team All-American in both his sophomore and junior seasons, and was a finalist for the Jim Thorpe Award, given annually to the nation's top defensive back.

Canty was so good he had the opportunity to leave K-State following his junior season, and took it.

"It was difficult to leave early," Canty said of his jump to the NFL. "It was a hard decision." Selected by the New England Patriots, Canty is currently playing for the Seattle Seahawks.

1. In addition to playing cornerback, what other position did Canty play in high school?

2. Canty was twice nominated for the College Defensive Back of the Year. Who is the award named after?

3. How many times was Canty named to the all-conference team?

4. How many interceptions did he return for touchdowns during his career at K-State?

5. How many interceptions did he have during the 1994 season?

6. How many career interceptions did he have for K-State?

7. Canty was an excellent punt returner. How many times did he return a punt for a touchdown?

8. In what round of the NFL Draft was he selected?

Lynn Dickey

Lynn Dickey
1968-70

The flagship player for Vince Gibson's "Purple Pride" teams from 1968-70, Lynn Dickey is the ultimate small-town Kansas boy made good. Passing up scholarship offers from KU and Missouri, Dickey found Manhattan – and the Wildcats – much to his liking.

K-State football fans were rather fond of him, too.

For three seasons, Dickey filled the air with passes, breaking school and Big Eight records, many of which still stand today. He led K-State to its first win over Oklahoma in 35 years, the school's first win over KU in 15 seasons, and the Wildcats' upset win over Nebraska in 1968. He became known for his white shoes – just as Joe Namath was – and exuded a confidence that was contagious among his teammates.

Lynn Dickey was a winner.

When the All-Time All-Big Eight team was announced, Lynn Dickey was the first-team quarterback, an honor that speaks for itself, exemplifying how valuable he was to K-State, and how well thought of he was by the rest of the conference.

"If I had to say one guy that really sticks out in my mind it has to be Lynn Dickey," Gibson said of his star quarterback. "He had a lot of places he could have gone, and he came to K-State. That meant something."

Dickey had a long pro career following his stint at KSU, throwing for more than 21,000 yards in the NFL.

1. What is Dickey's hometown?

2. How many career touchdown passes did he throw for K-State?

3. How many passes did Dickey complete in his career?

4. How many touchdown passes did he throw in K-State's smashing 59-21 win over Oklahoma in 1969?

5. How many interceptions did Dickey throw during his career at K-State?

6. How many career yards passing does Dickey have?

7. How many times was Dickey named to the All-Big Eight First Team?

8. In what round of the NFL Draft was Dickey selected?

9. What two NFL teams did Dickey play for?

Steve Grogan

Steve Grogan
1972-74

The big passing numbers that are usually associated with great quarterbacks are absent from Steve Grogan's career statistics. But Grogan, who ranks just 10th among the Wildcats' all-time passing leaders, wasn't about statistics. He was a football gamer, a big, tough quarterback who was just as comfortable running the ball as throwing it. And Grogan was a leader. For K-State fans, it is his leadership and determined playing style that is remembered.

Another product of small-town Kansas, Grogan didn't have the talent level around him other great K-State quarterbacks had. The Wildcats won just nine games in 1973-74, but it would have been a lesser total without Grogan.

"Anyone who played at K-State during those years, when we weren't winning many, had a lot of character," Grogan said of his playing days. He might of had the most.

Vince Gibson, Grogan's coach at K-State, always thought of his quarterback as a winner. And it is Grogan's experience at K-State, the bad beatings the team took from Oklahoma and Nebraska every season, that he attributes to the success he had in the NFL. He was a winner, regardless of what the won-lost column says of the teams he led at Kansas State.

1. Where did Grogan attend high school?

2. How many yards passing did Grogan have at K-State?

3. How many touchdown passes did he have?

4. How many yards rushing did Grogan have at K-State?

5. How many touchdowns did Grogan run for during his career at K-State?

6. Grogan wore number 11 at K-State. What number did he wear in the NFL?

7. In what round of the NFL Draft was Grogan selected?

8. How many different teams did he play for in the NFL?

Kevin Lockett

Kevin Lockett
1993-96

Great hands, terrific speed and an acrobatic flair for making great catches in tough situations. Kevin Lockett dazzled K-State fans for four seasons, and in the process helped the Wildcats reach for the top of the college football world. For what Lockett meant to K-State's football fortunes, he is equally reverent about what the school means to him.

"Choosing K-State is probably the best decision I ever made in my life," Lockett said of playing for the Wildcats and Coach Snyder.

Lockett finished his career as the all-time leader in receptions in the Big Eight, and was second on the charts in yardage with 3,032. He averaged 14 yards per catch. In addition to his athletic prowess, Lockett was a standout in the classroom and earned Academic All-American honors twice.

Lockett was selected by the Kansas City Chiefs in the 1997 NFL Draft, and has played three seasons in the NFL.

1. What high school in Tulsa, Oklahoma, did Lockett attend?

2. Lockett is KSU's all-time leading receiver. Who is number two on the Wildcats' all-time list?

3. How many touchdowns did Lockett score in his career at K-State?

4. His senior season, 1996, was his best at KSU. How many passes did he catch?

5. Three times during his career Lockett was a candidate to win a prestigious national award for his performance at wide receiver for the Wildcats. What's the name of this award?

6. How many career receptions does Lockett have?

7. In what round of the NFL Draft was Lockett selected?

8. Lockett wore number 83 at K-State. What number does he wear for the Kansas City Chiefs?

Jaime Mendez

Jaime Mendez
1990-93

The outstanding free safety from Ohio almost didn't stick around long enough to see the pendulum swing the other way for K-State. A redshirt in 1989, Mendez had a hard time dealing with the losing, but once the Wildcats snapped their 30-game winless streak, Mendez saw that a turn around was in progress, and then helped it along with his superb play.

The Big Eight's Defensive Newcomer of the Year in 1990, Mendez was a mainstay in the Wildcats' defensive backfield for four seasons, and he finished his career as K-State's all-time leader in interceptions. A perennial all-conference player in the Big Eight, Mendez was an unanimous first-team All-American his senior season in 1993. He finished his career as the ninth-leading tackler in K-State history with 313 stops.

Mendez had a brief pro football career after he left K-State.

1. Where did Mendez attend high school?

2. How many interceptions did he have his freshman season?

3. How many interceptions did he have for his career?

4. How many times was Mendez selected to the All-Big Eight Conference first team?

5. How many touchdowns did he score in his career?

6. In what round of the NFL Draft was Mendez selected?

7. What team did he play with his rookie season in the NFL?

8. He played two games in the CFL. Which team did he play for?

Gary Spani

Gary Spani
1974-77

His hits were ferocious and often. As K-State's middle linebacker for four seasons, Gary Spani put pain on the opposing runners and receivers who crossed his path on the field. The 6-foot-2, 222-pound linebacker averaged more than 12 tackles per game, an amazing number – an unbelievable number. The total tackles for his career is far above all other totals behind him.

"When you consider his range, instinct, and consistency," his coach, Ellis Rainsberger, said, "then you have to think of Spani in the same breath with the all-time great college linebackers."

Unfortunately, K-State was not very good during Spani's career. The team won only 10 games in four seasons, and just one conference game.

"We were an excellent defensive team most of my career," Spani said. "But we never scored any points."

An All-Big Eight performer throughout his career, Spani was K-State's first consensus All-American is senior season. He was a high selection in the NFL Draft and played in the pros for 10 seasons.

1. Where did Spani play high school football?

2. How many times was he selected to the All-Big Eight Conference first team?

3. How many total tackles did he have in his career?

4. Name two of the four groups that named Spani a first team All-American.

5. Spani shares the single-season tackle record with another player. Who is the player?

6. In what round of the NFL Draft was Spani selected?

7. What team drafted him?

8. How many seasons did he play in the NFL?

Percell Gaskins

Percell Gaskins

1993-95

Percell Gaskins took the long road to Manhattan, transferring to K-State after playing one season at an NAIA school. A powerful linebacker with blazing speed and incredible strength, Gaskins excelled on an impressive defensive unit for K-State. He racked up impressive tackle numbers, and led the team in stops in 1995. Gaskins was selected as a second-team All-American his senior year.

"I can give credit to hard-nosed work habits," Gaskins said of his success as an athlete. "Even as a little kid I was one who always worked hard."

Gaskins played in three bowl games for K-State, and collected six tackles in the Aloha Bowl against Boston College.

He was a third-round pick in the NFL Draft following his senior season.

1. Where did Gaskins attend high school?

2. What college did Gaskins play for before transferring to K-State?

3. What event did Gaskins win at the NCAA Track & Field Championships?

4. How many times was Gaskins selected to the All-Big Eight Conference first team?

5. How many tackles did he have in his career at K-State?

6. What team selected Gaskins in the 1995 NFL Draft?

7. How many teams has Gaskins played for in the NFL?

Ralph Graham

Ralph Graham
1931-33

"Running Ralph" was a scoring machine for K-State, a 6-foot-1 1/2, 205-pound fullback who totaled 196 points in his career from 1931-33. An All-Big Six selection three straight years, Graham tallied 85 points for the Cats in 1932. Unfortunately, a lack of accurate rushing records for the time period have kept his yardage totals a mystery, but it is known that he ran for 115 yards against Oklahoma in 1933.

Graham also possessed great leadership qualities, and led K-State to an impressive 18-8-1 record during his three-year career. A true gamer, Graham played almost non-stop, and logged an incredible 417 of a possible 480 minutes of playing time in 1933. After his brilliant career, Graham became an assistant coach at Indiana before returning to Kansas to become Wichita University's head coach. After leading the Wheatshockers to their first-ever bowl game in 1947, Graham returned to Manhattan and coached the Wildcats for three seasons.

He was elected to the Kansas Sports Hall of Fame in 1972.

1. Where did Graham play high school football?

2. What other sport did Graham excel in at K-State?

3. Two other colleges wanted Graham to play football for them. Who were these two schools?

4. How many touchdowns did Graham score for K-State?

5. How many extra points did Graham kick during his career?

6. How many seasons did Graham coach at Wichita, and what was his record there?

7. Graham led Wichita University to its first-ever bowl game following the 1947 season. What bowl game did the Shockers play in?

8. What was Graham's record as K-State's head coach?

Martin Gramatica

Martin Gramatica
1994-98

The joy of kicking. Nothing sums up Martin Gramatica's passion for his trade more than just watching him kick the football; following the high, powerful arc of the ball as it speeds toward the goalposts, and then Gramatica's elated, trademark happiness jump when the official raises his arm to signal that yes, of course it's good.

Gramatica jumped a lot when he was K-State.

"I just love to see the ball go through the uprights," Gramatica said of his celebration jumping. "It just takes me over."

After choosing the Wildcats over Michigan State and Notre Dame, Gramatica embarked on a kicking career that eclipsed all records at the school, as well as a few in the conference and nation. He holds the K-State records for most field goals in a game, season and career. Gramatica was a first-team All-American twice, and following his brilliant career, was selected in the third round of the 1999 NFL Draft.

1. Where was Gramatica born?

2. What is Gramatica's nickname?

3. How many field goals did Gramatica make in his career at K-State?

4. What was his percentage for made field goals?

5. Gramatica made the longest field goal in NCAA history without the use of a tee. How long was it, and who was the kick against?

6. Gramatica established an NCAA record for points scored by a kicker in 1998. How many points did he score?

7. How many points did Gramatica score in his career?

8. What prestigious award did Gramatica win in 1997?

9. Which NFL team drafted Gramatica?

Veryl Switzer

Veryl Switzer
1951-53

One of Kansas State's all-time great athletes, Veryl Switzer sped his way through opposing defenses and kick coverage squads, but also exerted a little physical power in his running, too. He was K-State's leading rusher for two seasons, and topped the nation in punt return average in 1953. But in addition to honing and elevating his football talents, Switzer had to overcome the ugly, racist attitudes that prevailed throughout the country in the 1950s.

"I hadn't put much thought into the race issue," Switzer said of his going to K-State, "because I didn't realize the restrictions on blacks competing at that level … I didn't anticipate any problems."

Just the second African-American on an athletic scholarship at K-State, Switzer endured hateful racial slurs, non-admittance to restaurants and hotels when the team traveled, and vicious hits from opposing players. Not only did he endure the weight of society's ills, he excelled.

"I was a pioneer and I understood that, so it (the racist attitudes) didn't bother me," Switzer said.

A first-team All-American in 1953, and a second-team All-American selection in 1952, he was taken as the third choice overall in the 1953 NFL Draft, the highest any K-State player has ever been chosen. Switzer played two seasons in the NFL and three in the CFL.

1. Where did Switzer attend high school?

2. What event did Switzer win in the 1952 Big Seven Indoor Track Championships?

3. What position did Switzer play on defense?

4. How many punt returns did Switzer run back for touchdowns during his K-State career?

5. Switzer led the nation in average yards per punt return in 1953. What was his average?

6. How many touchdowns did Switzer score in 1953?

7. Switzer ran back a punt 93 yards for a touchdown in 1953. Which team was this return against?

8. What NFL team drafted Switzer in 1953?

Henry Cronkite

Henry Cronkite
1929-31

Huge in size for his day, Henry Cronkite stood a full 6-foot-5 and weighed more than 200 pounds when he played football for the Kansas State Wildcats. Hailing from tiny Belle Plain, Kansas, Cronkite was a force on both offense and defense, and usually played every play of a game.

One of his best efforts was his performance against Nebraska in 1930. K-State had yet to defeat the Cornhuskers in 14 tries going into the contest, but Cronkite led the way to a 10-9 victory over the Cornhuskers, intercepting a pass as well as scoring the game's only touchdown. He also kicked a field goal and the extra point to account for all of the Wildcats' points.

An All-American selection in 1931 – when K-State finished with an impressive 8-2 record – Cronkite had a brief career in the NFL before returning to Kansas to coach high school football.

Henry Cronkite died on December 26, 1949.

1. Cronkite had decided to go to another college, but changed his mind and became a Wildcat instead. What school did he shun for K-State?

2. Cronkite played and lettered in two other sports at K-State. What were the sports?

3. Name three of the 10 organizations that selected Cronkite as an All-American in 1931.

4. What was Cronkite's primary position during his career at K-State?

5. How many times was he selected to the Big Six All-Conference team?

6. What NFL team did Cronkite play for?

Elmer Hackney

Elmer Hackney
1937-39

A big strapping runner with excellent speed, Elmer Hackney might be the greatest athlete to have ever graced the K-State campus. He was highly recognized throughout the Big Six Conference and around the country as one of the most powerful runners of his day. Sadly, the lack of records for the football team from his playing days leave little hint of his greatness.

Hackney had a great game against Washburn in 1938, bulling his way for two touchdowns. He also tallied a touchdown against Iowa State that same season.

He was a great shot putter, and held the American record after tossing the steel ball 55 feet, 11 inches at the national meet.

After finishing his career at K-State, Hackney played in the NFL for seven seasons. He died in 1969 at the age of 52.

1. Hackney had three nicknames. What were they?

2. Hackney made the 1940 Olympic team. Why didn't he compete in the Olympics?

3. How many times was he selected to the Big Six All-Conference first team?

4. Hackney missed most of the 1939 football season. What happened?

5. In what round of the NFL Draft was Hackney selected?

6. What team drafted him?

7. How many NFL teams did he play for?

8. How many yards rushing did he have in his NFL career?

Ray Hahn

Ray Hahn
1918, 1920-22

A product of the state of Kansas, Ray Hahn was the first K-State football player to be selected as an All-American. An excellent, athletic player, Hahn stood 5-foot-10 and weighed 190 pounds. An end for the Wildcats, Hahn was also the captain of the team in 1922, and was an instrumental part of K-State's 5-1-2 record that season. Twice he was named to the All-Missouri Valley Conference team.

He played briefly in the NFL, and returned to Kansas, where he coached high school and college athletics until 1974. He died in 1989.

1. What was Hahn's hometown in Kansas?

2. Hahn came to K-State in 1918. Why?

3. What organization or news service selected him as an All-American in 1922?

4. What pro team did Hahn play for?

5. Hahn started his coaching career at which Kansas high school?

6. What sport did Hahn coach at Bethany College for 36 years?

Cornelius Davis

Cornelius Davis
1966-68

As K-State's feature back on a dismal 1966 team, Cornelius Davis established himself as one of the top runners in the Big Eight Conference. Just a sophomore, Davis gained a total of 1,028 yards rushing – best in the Big Eight – scored six touchdowns and averaged 4.9 yards per carry. Surprisingly, he was left off the All-Conference first team. He gained more than 100 yards rushing in five games.

That 1966 season proved to be his high-water mark though, and Davis didn't approach the 1,000-yard mark for a season again. He finished his career as K-State's all-time leading rusher, and is still in the top 10 on that list.

Davis was selected in the fifth round of the 1969 NFL Draft.

1. What was Davis' nickname?

2. How many yards rushing did Davis have in his career at K-State?

3. How many touchdowns did he score in his career?

4. He ran for more than 100 yards in a game five times. What was his best total, and who did he do it against?

5. How many Big Eight All-Conference teams was he selected to?

6. What team selected him in the 1969 NFL Draft?

Mack Herron

Mack Herron
1968-69

An absolute mighty mite from Chicago, Mack Herron was short on stature, tall on talent. The speedy running back and return specialist stood just 5-foot-5, but because he was also a solid 170 pounds, he possessed an uncanny ability to maintain his balance and actually power through some tackles. But it was quickness, moves and speed that Herron used most often to accumulate yardage.

He also set a few records.

Herron led the Wildcats in rushing and receiving in 1969, as well as setting the school record for most points scored in a season. He finished with 3,150 total yards, and scored 188 points. Twice Herron returned kickoffs for touchdowns, and he also ran a punt back all the way for a score. He was a first-team All-Big Eight selection his senior season.

Following his career at K-State, Herron had a productive stint in the NFL.

1. What community college did Herron play for before coming to K-State?

2. How many touchdowns did Herron score in 1969?

3. How many total yards rushing did he have in his career?

4. What was the kickoff return average for his career?

5. He led the Wildcats in receiving in 1969. How many passes did he catch, and for how many yards?

6. In which round of the 1970 NFL Draft was he selected?

7. Who was the first pro team he played for?

8. How many NFL teams did he play for?

Clarence Scott

Clarence Scott
1968-70

A native Georgian, Clarence Scott came to K-State, and to fill a need on the defense, made the transition from offense to the defensive backfield. And he became a star.

The 6-foot, 190-pound Scott excelled beyond any possible expectations his coaches might have had for him, and by the end of his senior season in Manhattan he was a first-team All-American.

"Quickness is the main thing a good defensive back must have," Scott said in 1970. "It can make up for a lack of great speed." Scott used his quickness to finish his career at K-State with 12 interceptions, at the time a school record. His excellent one-on-one coverage was responsible for his good numbers.

Following his Wildcat career, Scott played for 13 seasons in the NFL.

1. Where did Scott attend high school?

2. What position was Scott originally slated to play at K-State?

3. An All-American in 1970, how many interceptions did Scott have that season?

4. How many touchdowns did he have in his career?

5. In what round of the 1971 NFL Draft was Scott selected?

6. How many teams did he play for in the NFL?

7. How many interceptions did Scott have in his NFL career?

Andre Coleman

Andre Coleman
1990-93

He was always dangerous when the ball was in his hands, possessing great breakaway speed and soft hands. Andre Coleman set Wildcats' fans in frenzies over his kick returns, and by his senior season in Manhattan the wide receiver was also making big plays with the offense.

For his career, Coleman averaged 24.3 yards per kickoff return. But it was when he began returning punts his senior year that the speedy Coleman came into his own; he averaged 13.4 yards per return on 27 runbacks that season.

1993 was also a breakout year of sorts for his receiving prowess. Coleman hauled in 42 passes that season, the most of his career, and he also scored six touchdowns. He was named a first-team All-Big Eight Conference selection following his '93 performance.

Coleman was drafted in the third round of the 1994 NFL Draft and has had a productive career in the NFL.

1. Where did Coleman attend high school?

2. How many kickoffs did he return for touchdowns during his career at KSU?

3. How many punts did he return for touchdowns during his career?

4. How many receiving yards did Coleman have in his career?

5. How touchdown passes did Coleman catch in his career?

6. Which team selected Coleman in the 1994 NFL Draft?

7. How many different NFL teams has Coleman played for?

Mark Simoneau

Mark Simoneau
1996-99

One of the best all-around athletes to play at K-State, Mark Simoneau was the model of consistency for the Wildcats throughout his career. The Smith Center, Kansas, native gathered awards and honors almost as much as he made tackles for the Wildcats, and was a major reason K-State sported one of the nation's top defenses from 1996 through 1999.

In addition to his defensive toughness and skills, Simoneau was the second player in the history of K-State football to be selected a three-time team captain. He finished third on K-State's all-time tackles chart following an outstanding season that saw him earn All-American honors. Other awards on the Simoneau shelf include Butkus Award Finalist, Big 12 All-Conference honors, and three Big 12 Defensive Player of the Week awards.

Following his great career at K-State, Simoneau was a high draft pick in the 2000 NFL Draft and looks to have a bright future in the pros.

1. How many times was Simoneau selected to the All-Big 12 first team?

2. How many interceptions did he have in his career?

3. How many total tackles did Simoneau have in his career at K-State?

4. Simoneau was the third consecutive K-State player chosen as the Defensive Freshman of the Year in the Big 12. Who were the first Wildcats to earn this honor?

5. How many seasons did Simoneau lead the team in tackles?

6. In which round of the 2000 NFL Draft was Simoneau selected? Which team selected him?

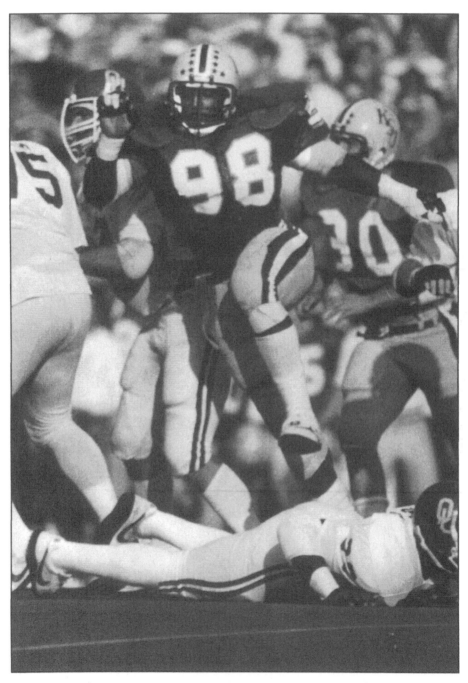

Reggie Singletary

Reggie Singletary
1980-83

Strong, powerful Reggie Singletary made one of the most immediate impacts a single player can make on a team when he joined the Wildcats in 1981.

"There's only one thing wrong with Reggie," his coach, Jim Dickey, said of his great defensive tackle. "There aren't enough of him. Could you imagine if we had three or four Reggies?"

Opposing teams refused to run his way, and still he made stops. Singletary – 6-foot-1 and 255 pounds – was routinely double-teamed throughout his career. He still set the K-State record for most tackles for a loss. He was the hands down Big Eight Defensive Newcomer of the Year in 1981, and being named to the Big Eight All-Conference team became an annual honor for him. He was also a tremendous force on the 1982 Independence Bowl team.

Unfortunately, Singletary never received the national acclaim he should have, and was never named to an All-American team. Still, he remains one of K-State's greatest defensive players.

1. What junior college did Singletary play at before coming to K-State?

2. How many career tackles did Singletary have at the end of his career at K-State?

3. How tackles for a loss did he have in his career?

4. Singletary switched to a different position the second half of his senior season. What was the position?

5. How many times was he on the All-Big Eight Conference first team?

6. In which round of the NFL Draft was Singletary selected?

Sean Snyder

Sean Snyder

1991-92

A booming, gifted punter, it was K-State's good fortune that Sean Snyder wanted to come to Manhattan. Of course that good fortune was born through Coach Bill Snyder, Sean's dad, but Sean developed into one of the top punters in the country. He became a tremendous weapon for the Wildcats.

"If he (Bill Snyder) wasn't sure it was the right move," Sean said of his dad's decision to bring him to K-State, "he wouldn't have done it, bottom line."

Snyder transferred from Iowa, and after sitting out a season, had two years of eligibility left. His first season he averaged 40.5 yards per punt. But in his senior season, Snyder raised his output considerably and averaged 44.7 yards per punt. And that was good enough to put him on the All-American first team.

Snyder had a brief stint in the NFL and is now an assistant athletic director at K-State.

1. Snyder played in one bowl game. Which one was it?

2. What was his career punting average at K-State?

3. How many times was he selected to the All-Big Eight team?

4. How many times did Snyder punt in 1992?

5. Snyder played in two all-star games. Which ones were they?

6. Snyder signed as a free agent with an NFL team following his career at K-State. Who was the team?

Chad May

Chad May
1993-94

Chad May, arm cocked high and ready to sling the football, rifled passes for two seasons at Kansas State and in just 22 games virtually re-wrote the school's record book. Consider: May broke the records for most passing yards in a game and season, touchdown passes in a career, most completions in a game and season, completion percentage and passing efficiency. Not enough? K-State was 18-5-1 with May behind center, and he also led the Cats to their first-ever bowl win.

May transferred to Kansas State and had to sit out the 1992 season, but when he took over the quarterbacking duties in 1993, K-State's football fortunes landed in the Top 20, and the Cats have been there ever since.

May had a monster senior season in 1994, completing almost 60 percent of his attempts and tossing 18 touchdown passes. He threw just five interceptions, and attempted 148 passes in '94 before one was finally picked off. He was first-team All-American in 1994

May was selected in the fourth round of the 1995 NFL draft.

1. Which school did May attend before transferring to K-State?

2. How many career passing yards does May have?

3. How many career touchdown passes does May have?

4. How many interceptions did May throw in his career?

5. How many touchdown passes did May throw in the 1993 Copper Bowl?

6. Which NFL team selected May in the 1995 Draft?

George Maddox

George Maddox
1932-34

The big Texan was one of Kansas State's first great linemen, and with his ferocious blocking and tackling skills, helped the Wildcats capture the 1934 Big Six championship. He stood 6-foot-3 and weighed 240 pounds, huge by the standards of his day. But more importantly, Maddox's leadership as the '34 team captain provided that extra intangible ingredient necessary for a championship team.

"Added responsibilities frequently develop new and valuable qualities in a football player," Christy Walsh, chairman of the All-American Board said in 1934. "George Maddox was a sterling tackle last year, but aside from his improved physical qualities this year – in the role of captain he had led his teammates through a hard schedule – eventually winning a championship title for the first time in the history of the Big Six Conference. . . He has been used to open holes for attacks, especially when yardage was badly needed-and he seldom failed to clear the path."

Maddox was the second K-State football player selected as a first-team All-American. He was also selected for every Big Six all-star team following the 1934 season. Maddox had a brief pro football career, and died on March 14, 1956, in McKinney, Texas.

1. What was Maddox's nickname?

2. Where did Maddox go to high school?

3. Three different sources selected Maddox as a first-team All-American in 1934. Who were the three sources?

4. How many football letters did Maddox win at K-State?

5. Which pro football team did Maddox play for?

6. How many games did he play in the NFL?

David Allen

David Allen
1997-2000

He can single-handily turn a game upside down, and he's done so several times. An electrifying game-breaker, David Allen has returned punts for touchdowns that have broken the opposing team's back and opened the door for a K-State win. His speed, moves and agile use of his blockers have made him the greatest kick returner in Kansas State history, and probably all of college football's history as well.

The two-time All-American needed just 172 yards in punt returns in his senior season to break one of the oldest NCAA records: Vanderbilt's Lee Nalley had 1,695 return yards from 1947-49. He is also one touchdown return away from owning that record by himself, as well. Allen was the first player in NCAA history to return punts for touchdowns in three consecutive games.

Not just a return man, Allen is also a more than capable running back, and looks to be the Wildcats top runner in the 2000 season.

1. Where did Allen attend high school?

2. What is his career punt return average?

3. How many kickoffs has Allen returned for touchdowns?

4. Allen holds the season punt return average record. What is it?

5. How many yards rushing does Allen have in his career?

6. How many touchdowns has Allen scored in his career?

7. How many times has Allen been selected for the Big 12 All-Conference first team?

David Allen celebrates after scoring in the 1998 Alamo Bowl.

Wildcat
Numbers

Rushing Records

Most Attempts
Game   41, Bill Butler vs. BYU, 9/25/71
Season   232, J.J. Smith, 1994
Career   507, Eric Hickson, 1994-98

Most Yards Gained
Long Rush 96, Gerald Hackney vs. Kansas, 11/2/48
Game   252, Mike Lawrence vs. Iowa State, 11/23/96
Season   1,137, Isaac Jackson, 1973
Career   2,537, Eric Hickson, 1994-98

Most Rushing Touchdowns
Game   4, Pat Jackson vs. New Mexico State, 9/15/90
Season   14, Bill Butler, 1971 & Michael Bishop, 1998
Career   26, Eric Hickson, 1994-98

Rushing Yards, Season

	Att	Yds	TD
1. Isaac Jackson, 1973	225	1,137	8
2. Eric Gallon, 1991	224	1,102	9
3. J.J. Smith, 1994	232	1,073	10
4. Cornelius Davis, 1966	210	1,028	6
5. Mike Lawrence, 1996	209	982	10

Rushing Yards, Career

	Att	Yds	TD
1. Eric Hickson, 1994-98	507	2,537	26
2. Mike Lawrence, 1994-97	492	2,265	19
3. J.J. Smith, 1991-94	491	2,210	22
4. Isaac Jackson, 1971-73	492	2,182	16
5. Eric Gallon, 1989-92	447	1,960	12

Passing Records

Most Attempts
Game	61, Lynn Dickey vs. Colorado, 11/22/69
Season	372, Lynn Dickey, 1969
Career	994, Lynn Dickey, 1968-70

Most Completions
Game	33, Chad May at Kansas, 10/6/94
Season	200, Chad May, 1994
Career	501, Lynn Dickey, 1968-70

Most Yards Gained
Play	97, Michael Bishop to Aaron Lockett vs. NE Louisiana, 9/26/98 95, Lane Brown to Francis Starns vs. Colorado, 10/20/51
Game	489, Chad May at Nebraska, 10/16/93
Season	2,844, Michael Bishop, 1998
Career	6,208, Lynn Dickey, 1968-70

Most Touchdown Passes
Game	4, Paul Watson vs. Louisiana Tech, 10/1/88; Chad May vs. Iowa State, 11/5/94; Brian Kavanagh vs. Colorado State, 12/29/95; Kavanagh vs. Rice, 9/21/96; Kavanagh vs. Oklahoma, 10/26/96; Kavanagh vs. Kansas, 11/9/96; Michael Bishop vs. Northern Illinois, 9/6/97; Bishop vs. Syracuse, 12/31/97; Bishop vs. NE Louisiana, 9/26/98; Jonathan Beasley vs. Oklahoma State, 10/23/99
Season	23, Michael Bishop, 1998
Career	36, Michael Bishop, 1997-98

Passing Yards, Season

	Att	Cmp	Yds	TD
1. Michael Bishop, 1998	295	164	2,844	23
2. Chad May, 1993	350	185	2,682	16
3. Chad May, 1994	337	200	2,571	18
4. Lynn Dickey, 1969	372	196	2,476	14
5. Paul Watson, 1991	304	172	2,354	10

Passing Yards, Career

	Att	Cmp	Yds	TD
1. Lynn Dickey, 1968-70	994	501	6,208	29
2. Chad May, 1993-94	687	385	5,253	34
3. Carl Straw, 1987-90	833	448	5,223	19
4. Michael Bishop, 1997-98	480	244	4,401	36
5. Darrell Dickey, 1979-82	640	319	4,098	23

Touchdown Passes, Season

1. Michael Bishop, 1998	23
2. Matt Miller, 1995	22
3. Brian Kavanagh, 1996	20
4. Chad May, 1994	18
5 Chad May, 1993	16

Touchdown Passes, Career

1. Michael Bishop, 1997-98	36
2. Chad May, 1993-94	34
3. Lynn Dickey, 1968-70	29
4. Brian Kavanagh, 1993-96	25
5. Darrell Dickey, 1979-82	23

Receiving Records

Most Receptions
Game	13, Michael Smith vs. Missouri, 10/21/89
Season	75, Darnell McDonald, 1998
Career	217, Kevin Lockett, 1993-96

Most Yards Gained
Play	97, Aaron Lockett from Michael Bishop vs. NE Louisiana, 9/26/98
	95, Francis Starns from Lane Brown vs. Colorado, 10/20/51
Game	206, Darnell McDonald vs. Syracuse, 12/31/97
Season	1,092, Darnell McDonald, 1998
Career	3,032, Kevin Lockett, 1993-96

Most Touchdowns Receptions
Game	3, John Williams vs. Austin Peay State, 9/5/87; Michael Smith vs. Iowa State, 11/9/91; Jimmy Dean at Rice, 9/21/96; Darnell McDonald vs. Syracuse, 12/31/97
Season	13, Kevin Lockett, 1995
Career	26, Kevin Lockett, 1993-96

Most Receptions, Single Game
	Name, Opponent, Date	Re-Yds
1.	Michael Smith vs. Missouri, 10/21/89	13-166
2.	Darnell McDonald vs. Nebraska, 11/13/98	12-183
	Kevin Lockett vs. Oklahoma, 10/26/96	12-157
	Michael Smith vs. Washington, 9/28/91	12-174
	Mack Herron vs. Colorado, 11/22/69	12-171

Receptions, Season
		Rec	Yds	TD
1.	Darnell McDonald, 1998	75	1,092	9
2.	Kevin Lockett, 1996	72	882	6
3.	Michael Smith, 1989	70	816	2
4.	Greg Washington, 1988	69	928	9
5.	John Goerger, 1972	57	612	1

Receiving Yards, Season

		Rec	Yds	Avg
1.	Darnell McDonald, 1998	75	1,092	14.6
2.	Quincy Morgan	42	1,007	24.0
3.	Greg Washington, 1988	69	928	13.4
	Aaron Lockett, 1998	44	928	21.1
5.	Kevin Lockett, 1996	72	882	12.3

Pass Receptions, Career

		Rec	Yds	TD
1.	Kevin Lockett, 1993-96	217	3,032	26
2.	Michael Smith, 1988-91	179	2,457	11
3.	Mitch Running, 1992-95	133	1,821	10
4.	Dave Jones, 1966-68	127	1,904	5
5.	Frank Hernandez, 1988-91	120	1,489	9

Scoring Records

Most Points

Game	28, Ralph Graham (4 TD, 4 PAT) vs. Kansas Wesleyan, 10/7/32
	24, Ralph Graham vs. Wichita, 9/24/31;
	Graham vs. KSTC, Emporia, 9/30/33;
	Mack Herron vs. Missouri, 11/1/69;
	Bill Butler vs. Oklahoma, 10/23/71;
	Pat Jackson, vs. New Mexico State, 9/15/90
Season	135, Martin Gramatica, 1998
Career	349, Martin Gramatica, 1994-98

Most Touchdowns

Game	4, Ralph Graham vs. Wichita, 9/24/31;
	Graham vs. Kansas Wesleyan, 10/7/32;
	Graham vs. KSTC, Emporia, 9/30/33;
	Mack Herron vs. Missouri, 11/1/69;
	Bill Butler vs. Oklahoma, 10/23/71;
	Pat Jackson vs. New Mexico State, 9/15/90
Season	21, Mack Herron, 1969
Career	31, Mack Herron, 1968-69; Ralph Graham, 1931-33

Most Extra Points Kicked
Game	9, Martin Gramatica vs. Indiana State, 9/5/98; Jamie Rheem vs. Missouri, 11/13/99
Season	69, Martin Gramatica, 1998
Career	187, Martin Gramatica, 1994-98

Most Field Goals
Game	5, Jamie Rheem vs. Texas, 10/2/99 4, Martin Gramatica vs. Kansas, 10/31/98; Martin Gramatica vs. Texas A&M, 12/5/98
Season	22, Martin Gramatica, 1998
Career	54, Martin Gramatica, 1994-98

Scoring, Season
		Points
1.	Martin Gramatica, 1998	135
2.	Mack Herron, 1969	126
3.	Bill Butler, 1971	96
4.	Jamie Rheem, 1999	95
5.	Martin Gramatica, 1997	94

Scoring, Career
		Points
1.	Martin Gramatica, 1994-98	349
2.	Ralph Graham, 1931-33	196
	Tate Wright, 1990-93	196
4.	Mack Herron, 1968-69	188
5.	Steve Willis, 1981-84	187

Tackle Records

Tackles
Game	28, Danny Lankas vs. Missouri, 11/11/67
Season	178, Gary Spani, 1977; Danny Lankas, 1967
Career	543, Gary Spani, 1974-77
Freshman	111, Mark Simoneau, 1996

Powercat Numbers

Quarterback Sacks
Game	3, Nyle Wiren vs. Iowa State, 11/5/94;
	vs. Kansas, 10/28/95;
	vs. Texas Tech, 8/31/96;
	Jeff Kelly vs. Bowling Green, 9/27/97;
	Darren Howard vs. Iowa State, 11/22/97;
	Joe Bob Clements vs. Colorado, 10/10/98
Season	11.5, Nyle Wiren, 1996
Career	29.5, Darren Howard, 1996-99

Career Tackles Leaders
		Fr-So-Jr-Sr	=	Total
1.	Gary Spani, 1974-77	61-153-151-178	=	543
2.	Brooks Barta, 1989-92	81-105-108-142	=	436
3.	Mark Simoneau, 1996-99	111-103-95-91	=	400
4.	Theopilis Bryant, 1973-76	80-90-94-117	=	381
5.	Danny Lankas, 1965-67	X-10-175-178	=	363
6.	Dan Ruzich, 1979-82	3-75-131-150	=	359
7.	Carl Pennington, 1973-76	38-68-118-116	=	340
8.	Matt Wallerstedt, 1984-87	34-46-93-165	=	338
9.	Barton Hundley, 1981-82, '84-85	27-18-133-136	=	314
10.	Jaime Mendez, 1990-93	40-79-67-127	=	313

Quarterback Sacks, Career
		Sacks
1.	Darren Howard, 1996-99	29.5
2.	Nyle Wiren, 1993-96	27.5
3.	Dirk Ochs, 1992-95	24
4.	Tim Colston, 1992-95	18
5.	Mark Simoneau, 1996-99	15.5
6.	John Butler, 1990-93	14
7.	Jeff Kelly, 1997-98	13
8.	Jeffery Hurd, 1983-86	12
9.	Grady Newton, 1983-87	11
	Kevin Humphrey, 1985-86	11

Quarterback Sacks, Season

		Sacks
1.	Nyle Wiren , 1996	11.5
2.	Darren Howard, 1997	11
3.	Dirk Ochs, 1995	11
4.	Darren Howard, 1998	10.5
5.	John Butler, 1993	9
	Kevin Humphrey, 1985	9
7.	Tim Colston, 1995	8
	Nyle Wiren, 1994	8
	Dirk Ochs, 1993	8
	Dwayne Castille, 1984	8
11.	Tim Colston, 1994	7
	Nyle Wiren, 1995	7
	Jeff Kelly, 1997	7

K-State Football Season by Season

Year	Coach	W	L	T
1896	Ira Pratt	0	1	1
1897	A.W. Ehrsam	1	2	1
1898	W.P. Williamson	1	1	2
1899	Albert Hanson	2	3	0
1900	F.G. Moulton	2	4	0
1901	Wade Moore	3	4	1
1902	C.E. Dietz	2	6	0
1903	G.O. Dietz	3	4	1
1904	A.A. Booth	1	6	0
1905	Mike Ahearn	6	2	0
1906	Mike Ahearn	5	2	0
1907	Mike Ahearn	5	3	0
1908	Mike Ahearn	6	2	0
1909	Mike Ahearn	7	2	0
1910	Mike Ahearn	10	1	0
1911	Guy Lowman	5	4	1
1912	Guy Lowman	8	2	0
1913	Guy Lowman	3	4	1
1914	Guy Lowman	1	5	1
1915	John R. Bender	3	4	1
1916	Z.G. Clevenger	6	1	1
1917	Z.G. Clevenger	6	2	0
1918	Z.G. Clevenger	4	1	0
1919	Z.G. Clevenger	3	5	1
1920	Charles Bachman	3	3	3
1921	Charles Bachman	5	3	0
1922	Charles Bachman	5	1	2
1923	Charles Bachman	4	2	2
1924	Charles Bachman	3	4	1
1925	Charles Bachman	5	2	1
1926	Charles Bachman	5	3	0
1927	Charles Bachman	3	5	0
1928	Bo McMillin	3	5	0
1929	Bo McMillin	3	5	0
1930	Bo McMillin	5	3	0
1931	Bo McMillin	8	2	0
1932	Bo McMillin	4	4	0

156

1933	Bo McMillin	6	2	1
1934	Lynn Waldorf	7	2	1
1935	Wes Fry	2	4	3
1936	Wes Fry	4	3	2
1937	Wes Fry	4	5	0
1938	Wes Fry	4	4	1
1939	Wes Fry	4	5	0
1940	Hobbs Adams	2	7	0
1941	Hobbs Adams	2	5	2
1942	Ward Haylett	3	8	0
1943	Ward Haylett	1	7	0
1944	Ward Haylett	2	5	2
1945	Lud Fiser	1	7	0
1946	Hobbs Adams	0	9	0
1947	Sam Francis	0	10	0
1948	Ralph Graham	1	9	0
1949	Ralph Graham	2	8	0
1950	Ralph Graham	1	9	1
1951	Bill Meek	0	9	0
1952	Bill Meek	1	9	0
1953	Bill Meek	6	3	1
1954	Bill Meek	7	3	0
1955	Bus Mertes	4	6	0
1956	Bus Mertes	3	7	0
1957	Bus Mertes	3	6	1
1958	Bus Mertes	3	7	0
1959	Bus Mertes	2	8	0
1960	Doug Weaver	1	9	0
1961	Doug Weaver	2	8	0
1962	Doug Weaver	0	10	0
1963	Doug Weaver	2	7	0
1964	Doug Weaver	3	7	0
1965	Doug Weaver	0	10	0
1966	Doug Weaver	0	9	1
1967	Vince Gibson	1	9	0
1968	Vince Gibson	4	6	0
1969	Vince Gibson	5	5	0
1970	Vince Gibson	6	5	0
1971	Vince Gibson	5	6	0
1972	Vince Gibson	3	8	0

Year	Coach			
1973	Vince Gibson	5	6	0
1974	Vince Gibson	4	7	0
1975	Ellis Rainsberger	3	8	0
1976	Ellis Rainsberger	1	10	0
1977	Ellis Rainsberger	2	9	0
1978	Jim Dickey	4	7	0
1979	Jim Dickey	3	8	0
1980	Jim Dickey	4	7	0
1981	Jim Dickey	2	9	0
1982	Jim Dickey	6	5	1
1983	Jim Dickey	3	8	0
1984	Jim Dickey	3	7	1
1985	Jim Dickey/Lee Moon	1	10	0
1986	Stan Parrish	2	9	0
1987	Stan Parrish	0	10	1
1988	Stan Parrish	0	11	0
1989	Bill Snyder	1	10	0
1990	Bill Snyder	5	6	0
1991	Bill Snyder	7	4	0
1992	Bill Snyder	5	6	0
1993	Bill Snyder	9	2	1
1994	Bill Snyder	9	3	0
1995	Bill Snyder	10	2	0
1996	Bill Snyder	9	3	0
1997	Bill Snyder	11	1	0
1998	Bill Snyder	11	2	0
1999	Bill Snyder	11	1	0

All-Time Coaches' Records

Coach	Years	Won	Lost	Ties	Pct.
Ira Pratt	1896	0	1	1	.250
A.W. Ehrsam	1897	1	2	1	.375
W.P. Williamson	1898	1	1	2	.500
Albert Hanson	1899	2	3	0	.400
F.G. Moulton	1900	2	4	0	.333
Wade Moore	1901	3	4	1	.438
C.E. Dietz	1902	2	6	0	.250
G.O. Dietz	1903	3	4	1	.438
A.A. Booth	1904	1	6	0	.143
Mike Ahearn	1905-10	39	12	0	.765
Guy Lowman	1911-14	17	15	3	.529
John Bender	1915	3	4	1	.438
Z.G. Clevenger	1916-19	19	9	2	.667
Charles Bachman	1920-27	33	23	9	.577
Bo McMillin	1928-33	29	21	1	.578
Lynn Waldorf	1934	7	2	1	.750
Wes Fry	1935-39	18	21	6	.467
Hobbs Adams	1940-41, 46	4	21	2	.185
Ward Haylett	1942-44	6	20	2	.250
Lud Fiser	1945	1	7	0	.125
Sam Francis	1947	0	10	0	.000
Ralph Graham	1948-50	4	26	1	.145
Bill Meek	1951-54	14	24	1	.372
Bus Mertes	1955-59	15	34	1	.310
Doug Weaver	1960-66	8	60	1	.123
Vince Gibson	1967-74	33	52	0	.388
Ellis Rainsberger	1975-77	6	27	0	.182
Jim Dickey	1978-85	25	53	2	.325
Lee Moon	1985	1	8	0	.111
Stan Parrish	1986-88	2	30	1	.076
Bill Synder	1989-99	88	40	1	.689
Totals	104 years	388	550	41	.414

Michael Bishop celebrates with teammates during the 1998 season.

More
Wildcat Trivia

Bill Snyder

Bill Snyder

Maybe the best thing about Bill Snyder's football renaissance at Kansas State is that it was built on a solid foundation.

"It's going to be one step at a time. There's not going to be any shortcuts," Coach Snyder said when he first arrived in Manhattan. "I'm not going to promise you we're going to win one, two, five, seven or 10. All I can promise you is we're going to get a little bit better every day."

K-State's football program had suffered from decades of infectious, contagious losing. But if losing is a disease, and it was at K-State, then Coach Snyder was the cure. He has had more winning seasons in his tenure as the Wildcats' top man – eight through the 1999 season – than the school had had in the previous 58 seasons before he arrived.

Amazing.

"There weren't any goals directed toward lifting the illness of losing," Snyder said of his rebuilding job, "it was just a matter of you get better, all the rest of the stuff will take care of itself."

And the Wildcats did get better. Did they ever.

After four step-by-step building years, K-State broke out with a 9-2-1 season in 1993, which included the school's first-ever bowl victory.

And they have stayed at that win level or better ever since.

K-State has appeared in seven straight bowls through 1999, and Coach Snyder has led the team to three 11-win years in a row. In the great 1998 season, the Wildcats earned their first-ever No. 1 ranking in the country's top polls, and only an overtime loss to Texas A&M kept the Cats from playing for the national championship.

Coach Snyder has re-written K-State's football history, expunging its losing past. To say he is the greatest coach in the Wildcats' history is so much more than an understatement; let's say he has been the greatest college football coach the past decade, which he has been.

1. Where did Coach Snyder graduate from college?

2. In what two states did Coach Snyder coach high school football?

3. Coach Snyder was an assistant to Hayden Fry at the University of Iowa. What school did he coach at before going to Iowa?

4. Who was the first Big Eight opponent to be defeated by Coach Snyder's Wildcats?

163

5. Which position did Coach Snyder play in college?

6. Coach Snyder has won virtually every coaching award possible since coming to K-State. When did he win his first National Coach of the Year Award?

7. Where did Coach Snyder first coach on a college level?

8. What is Coach Snyder's overall record at K-State through the 1999 season?

9. How many different head coaches did K-State have before Coach Snyder was hired in 1989?

10. How many head coaching jobs did Snyder have before coming to K-State?

K-State sideline at the 1997 Cotton Bowl.

Coach Snyder

Vince Gibson

Vince Gibson

When he arrived from Tennessee to take over K-State's head coaching job, Vince Gibson didn't mince words, make excuses, or ponder his situation. Instead, he made a bold prediction.

"We gonna win."

Gibson's squads never shook the foundation of the college football world, but he brought respectability to K-State's program, if only for a couple of the seven seasons he was in Manhattan. After decades of losing and losing big, Gibson's "Purple Pride" campaign paid off with a few big wins for Kansas State.

His first team won only one game, but when Lynn Dickey became his starting quarterback the following year, good things happened. K-State pulled a major upset in 1968 by defeating Nebraska, and finished the season strong with a win over Oklahoma State. The four-win season was the most a K-State team had had since 1955. And most importantly, the 1968 Wildcats became the first K-State team to ever be ranked in the Top 20.

Gibson's Wildcats defeated KU in 1969, the first time K-State had downed the Jayhawks since 1955. The '69 squad also smothered the Sooners, 59-21, one of the biggest wins in the history of the school.

The 1970 team finished 6-5 – including wins over Oklahoma and Colorado – and might have had a shot at a bowl game if the program hadn't been slapped with probation by the Big Eight Conference. The rest of Gibson's time in Manhattan was spent trying to stay out of the Big Eight's cellar, but he definitely made his mark on the history of K-State football.

Gibson left K-State following the 1974 season and became the head coach at Louisville the following season.

1. What was Gibson's overall record at K-State?

2. How many winning seasons did he have as K-State's head coach?

3. How many times did Gibson's teams defeat KU?

4. What was the highest finish one of his teams had in the Big Eight?

5. What's the highest ranking one of his teams had during his coaching career at K-State?

6. Which Big Eight school did Gibson defeat the most?

Jim Dickey

Jim Dickey

J im Dickey's career at K-State is best summed up by his redshirt scheme of 1981, when he sat down the majority of his senior players for one season to save them for the 1982 campaign.

"I noted that other teams' starting players were always a year or two older than us, and subsequently stronger and more mature," Dickey said of the plan. "When I suggested redshirting several of our veteran returning players, most of my assistants told me it wouldn't work and the players wouldn't go along."

But the players did go along, and after going 2-9 in 1981, the Wildcats' veteran players returned and gave K-State fans one of the school's best seasons to date, going 6-4-1 and earning a trip to the Independence Bowl. It was a taste of success Kansas State had never known before.

The rest of Dickey's career was a struggle, and he had no other winning seasons. But the one high-point season in his career is enough to make him an important figure in the history of K-State's head coaches.

Dickey resigned following the second game of the 1985 season, a 10-6 loss to Northern Iowa.

1. What was Dickey's overall record at K-State?

2. Who was the first team Dickey's Wildcats defeated?

3. How many times did Dickey's teams defeat KU?

4. Which Big Eight team did Dickey's Wildcats defeat the most times?

5. How many Top 20 teams did K-State defeat during Dickey's tenure?

6. Northern Iowa defeated K-State in Dickey's last game as head coach. Which school defeated K-State in the first game of the 1985 season?

Charles Bachman

Charles Bachman

When he arrived in Manhattan as the Wildcats' head football coach in 1920, Charles Bachman had already accomplished a lot in his football career. He played for Knute Rockne at Notre Dame, and had won the Rose Bowl as a coach. At Kansas State, Bachman returned the school's mascot name to Wildcats (from Farmers), had five winning seasons, and coached the school's first All-American, Ray Hahn.

His 1922 K-State team put together a fine season, posting a record of 5-1-2. Bachman's 1924 club was the first to defeat KU since 1906, and he didn't lose to the Jayhawks again the rest of his time in Manhattan. Bachman also never lost to Oklahoma.

After resigning from K-State, Bachman coached at Florida before moving on from there. He retired in 1946, and then coached one more season in 1953. Known for his offensive innovations, Bachman was the inventor of the "Flying Z" offense, and was also one of the first coaches to use liberal substitutions as a part of his game plan.

An honoree in the National Football Foundation Hall of Fame, Bachman was inducted into the K-State Sports Hall of Fame in 1995.

1. Bachman earned a law degree from which university?

2. One of Bachman's teams won the Rose Bowl game and national championship before he came to K-State. Who was the team?

3. Bachman coached at Florida after he left K-State. Which school did he coach after he left Florida?

4. How many winning seasons did Bachman have as K-State's coach?

5. Bachman came out of retirement and coached one more season in 1953. Which school did he coach at?

6. What was Bachman's overall record at K-State?

Coaches

Lynn "Pappy" Waldorf

Stan Parrish

![Bill Meek]

Bill Meek

1. Who was K-State's first football coach?

2. Bill Snyder is the all-time leader in K-State coaching victories with 88 (through 1999). Who is second in career wins among K-State's head football coaches?

3. A victory by K-State over Colorado in its final game of the 1954 season would have sent the Wildcats to Miami for the Orange Bowl. K-State lost the game, but still finished with a 7-3 record. Who was the head coach in 1954?

4. K-State had a different coach in 1946 and 1947. One coach went 0-9, the other 0-10. Who were these two coaches?

5. Lynn "Pappy" Waldorf coached just one season at K-State. What was the team's record that year?

6. Which school did Waldorf coach before he came to K-State?

7. Which school did Waldorf coach immediately after he left K-State?

8. K-State had an interim coach in 1985. Who was he, and what was his record?

9. How many Big Eight teams did Stan Parrish's teams defeat?

10. Doug Weaver was fired as K-State's head coach following the 1966 season after winning just eight games in seven seasons. Which school hired him as an assistant coach the following year?

Bowl Games

1982 Independence Bowl

Wisconsin 14, Kansas State 3
December 11, 1982
Shreveport, Louisiana

It was a long time coming, and the result was disappointing.

Kansas State's first-ever bowl appearance in its 87-year football history was met by miserable, wet weather and a determined Wisconsin Badgers team. Playing in a light drizzle, gusty winds and sub-zero temperatures throughout the game, the Wildcats weren't able to muster much of an offense and fell to the Badgers, 14-3.

K-State took the early lead on a 29-yard field goal by Steve Willis midway through the second quarter. The Badgers struck back quickly though, and went ahead, 7-3, less than three minutes later. A long pass play in the third quarter put Wisconsin up 14-3, and the Wildcats, led by quarterback Darrell Dickey, weren't able to rally.

Kansas State finished its first-ever bowl season with a 6-5-1 record.

1. Who was K-State's leading rusher in the game?

2. How many turnovers did Wisconsin have in the game?

3. How many yards passing did Dickey have in the game?

4. Who was K-State's leading tackler in the game?

5. The Badgers' quarterback threw two touchdown passes in the game. What's his name?

6. How many turnovers did K-State have in the game?

7. What was the attendance of the game?

K-State's Iosefatu Faraimo struggles for yardage in the 1982 Independence Bowl against Wisconsin.

1993 Copper Bowl

Kansas State 52, Wyoming 17
December 29, 1993
Tucson, Arizona

Riding a powerful offensive force throughout the game, Bill Snyder's Kansas State Wildcats ripped apart the Wyoming Cowboys in spectacular fashion, and recorded the school's first-ever bowl triumph.

Kansas State 52, Wyoming 17.

At least 20,000 K-State fans made the trip to Tucson, and they weren't disappointed. The Wildcats raced to a 24-10 lead at the half and never looked back during the last two quarters. The Cowboys were blitzed on all sides; K-State scored on long drives, long passes and short runs. They shut down Wyoming's running game, sacked the quarterback and collected three turnovers. When the game was over, K-State had more than 500 yards of total offense. It was, in short, a powerful display by the 20th-ranked Wildcats.

J. J. Smith led the K-State running attack, which finished the game with 227 yards. Chad May hit on 68 percent of his passes, and the special teams chipped in with a touchdown.

Kansas State finished the season ranked 20th in the AP poll, 18th in the CNN/USA Today poll.

1. How many different K-State players scored in the game?

2. How many yards passing did Chad May have in the game?

3. How many touchdown passes did May throw in the game?

4. How many yards rushing did J. J. Smith have?

5. Who was K-State's leading tackler in the game?

6. Andre Coleman scored two touchdowns in the game, one on a pass reception. How did he score the other touchdown?

7. The defensive standout recorded 11 tackles in the game and returned an interception 37 yards for Kansas State's last touchdown. Who is he?

8. How many yards of total offense did Kansas State have for the game?

Chad May runs into the end zone in second quarter action of the 1993 Copper Bowl.

9. Who won the offensive MVP honors for the game?

10. How many times did K-State sack Wyoming's quarterback?

1994 Aloha Bowl

Boston College 12, Kansas State 7
December 25, 1994
Honolulu, Hawaii

The Hawaii holiday ended on a sour note.

Facing a tough run defense and powerful pass rush, Kansas State was unable to muster much of an offense and lost a hard-fought game to the Boston College Eagles, 12-7.

This wasn't the way things were supposed to go.

Kansas State relinquished an early touchdown, but evened the score at the end of the first period. When Chad May was tackled in the end zone late in the second quarter, the Eagles led 9-7. The rest of the game saw K-State mired in offensive futility, but its defense kept the eighth-ranked Wildcats close. Boston College kicked a 35-yard field goal with 1:18 remaining in the game, but May had one last chance to pull out the game for the Wildcats. He almost did.

From the Eagles' 45-yard line and 10 seconds left in the game, May threw for the end zone – and the win – hoping Mitch Running could pull in the pass. The ball was knocked away and Boston College had the game, 12-7.

The loss dropped K-State's final ranking in the polls to 16th (CNN/USA Today)and 19th (AP).

1. How many yards rushing did K-State have in the game?

2. How many times did Boston College sack Chad May?

3. How did K-State score its touchdown?

4. Who was K-State's leading receiver?

5. How many times did K-State have to punt in the game?

6. Who was K-State's MVP of the game?

1995 Holiday Bowl

Kansas State 54, Colorado State 21
December 29, 1995
San Diego, California

Kansas State unleashed its impressive offensive juggernaut on the Colorado State Rams, and for the second time in three years, recorded a blowout win in a bowl game. The 10th-ranked Wildcats humbled the No. 25 ranked Rams from start to finish, and once again amassed more than 500 yards of total offense in the rout. In the end, the score reflected the dominance of K-State over its WAC opponent, 54-21.

K-State quarterback Matt Kavanagh – subbing for the injured Matt Miller – was superb, completing 75 percent of his passes. The Wildcats' defense – the top-ranked unit in the nation – was smothering, holding CSU to 169 yards rushing, gathering four turnovers and limiting the Rams to just six pass completions. It was a dominating team performance.

For his performance, Kavanagh was named the game's offensive MVP. Eric Hickson led the Wildcat running game, and Mitch Running was the team's top receiver in the game. The big win shot the Wildcats into the Top 10, and they finished as the sixth-ranked team in the CNN/USA Today poll, seventh in the AP poll.

1. Before he was injured, how many passes did Matt Miller complete?

2. How many touchdown passes did Kavanagh throw in the game?

3. How many yards of total offense did K-State have in the game?

4. How many yards rushing did Eric Hickson have in the game?

5. The Wildcats picked off three CSU passes in the game. Who made the interceptions for KSU?

6. Mitch Running had a great game. How many receiving yards did he have?

K-State's Kevin Lockett celebrates with teammates after scoring in the 1995 Holiday Bowl.

1997 Cotton Bowl

BYU 19, Kansas State 15
January 1, 1997
Dallas, Texas

The Wildcats roared into Dallas, and with the support of approximately 45,000 rabid K-State fans, played in their first-ever New Year's Day bowl game. The exciting, defense-dominated game left the purple-clad fans a little blue, though, as the fifth-ranked BYU Cougars staged a two-touchdown, fourth-quarter comeback and defeated K-State, 19-15.

The Wildcats fell behind in the first quarter when KSU quarterback Brian Kavanagh was sacked in the end zone for a safety. The Cougars added a field goal later to lead, 5-0. K-State took the lead on the final play of the first half, a 41-yard bomb that was deflected and caught for a touchdown. A two-point conversion gave K-State an 8-5 lead.

Kevin Lockett made a brilliant run following a short slant pattern reception to put the Wildcats up 15-5 in the third period, but BYU answered the bell in the fourth quarter, scoring twice on touchdown passes, the last one with just 3:39 remaining. K-State moved to the BYU 12-yard line with one minute remaining, but an interception by Omarr Morgan sealed the win for BYU.

Both teams had problems running the ball throughout the game, and sacks were numerous by both sides. K-State totaled 274 yards of total offense, BYU finished with 350. The loss dropped the Wildcats' record to 9-3, and finished as the 17th-ranked team in both polls.

1. Who scored K-State's first touchdown?

2. How long was Kevin Lockett's touchdown play in the third quarter?

3. How many times did K-State sack the BYU quarterback?

4. How many times was K-State quarterback Kavanagh sacked?

5. Who was K-State's leading rusher?

6. Who scored the two-point conversion following K-State's first touchdown?

180

Kevin Lockett just misses getting his foot down for a touchdown in the 1997 Cotton Bowl.

7. Two players shared the offensive MVP award for the game. Who were they?

8. How many yards receiving did Lockett have in the game?

1997 Fiesta Bowl

Kansas State 35, Syracuse 18
December 31, 1997
Tempe, Arizona

In a fitting conclusion to the Wildcats' finest football season to date in the history of the school, K-State disposed of the Big East's Syracuse Orangemen and won the Fiesta Bowl going away, 35-18.

For the first time, K-State finished the season with 11 wins.

K-State quarterback Michael Bishop played one of the best games of his career, completing 14 passes and accounting for all five of the Wildcats' touchdowns. Darnell McDonald was also brilliant, setting a school record for receiving yards on seven receptions. Bishop was also the team's leading rusher.

After Syracuse took a 3-0 lead in the first quarter, Bishop led the Wildcats on three touchdown drives in the second quarter. Syracuse closed the gap to 21-15 at the half, but two Bishop touchdown passes put the game away in the fourth quarter.

The bowl victory moved the Cats up in the final poll rankings, as they finished seventh in the coaches poll, and eighth in the AP poll.

1. How many touchdown passes did Michael Bishop have in the game?

2. How many yards receiving did Darnell McDonald have in the game?

3. Who was K-State's leading rusher?

4. Who scored K-State's only rushing touchdown?

5. How many times did Syracuse sack Bishop in the game?

6. Who was K-State's leading tackler?

K-State coach Bill Snyder accepts the trophy after the Wildcats win the 1997 Fiesta Bowl.

1998 Alamo Bowl

Purdue 37, Kansas State 34
December 29, 1998
San Antonio, Texas

It was a disappointing end to a spectacular season.

K-State, after flirting with national championship dreams most of the season, dropped an intense, exciting contest to Purdue. Shut out of a deserving spot in a major bowl off the heartbreaking loss to Texas A&M in the Big 12 Championship game, the Wildcats never found their collective playing rhythm against Purdue. 30,000 K-State fans watched in disappointment as a late Purdue touchdown snuffed away the Wildcats' comeback and won, 37-34.

After trailing most of the game, K-State quarterback Michael Bishop hit Justin Swift with a two-yard touchdown pass that put the Cats up 34-30. There was only 1:23 left in the game.

But Purdue, behind the passing of Drew Brees, moved 80 yards in six plays to score the game-winning touchdown with 30 seconds left in the game. Bishop was intercepted on K-State's final possession to wrap up the victory for Purdue.

K-State trailed 17-7 at the half, and 27-13 after three quarters. Bishop threw for 182 yards and three touchdowns, but his four interceptions matched his entire total for the season. The loss left K-State with an 11-2 record and a final ranking of ninth in the coaches poll and 10th in the AP poll.

1. Who was K-State's leading rusher in the game?

2. Who was K-State's leading receiver?

3. How did K-State score its second touchdown?

4. How many pass attempts did Purdue have in the game?

5. How many interceptions did K-State have?

6. How many times did KSU sack Purdue quarterback Drew Brees?

7. How many yards rushing did Purdue have in the game?

Michael Bishop gets off a pass against heavy Purdue pressure in the 1998 Alamo Bowl.

1999 Holiday Bowl

Kansas State 24, Washington 20
December 29, 1999
San Diego, California

Kansas State fought past the Washington Huskies and captured the 1999 Holiday Bowl the hard way: they earned it.

Led by quarterback Jonathan Beasley, K-State grounded out 92 yards in 20 plays to get the game-winning touchdown. The drive lasted 9:54.

"You wouldn't think it would take 20 plays to go the length of the field," Beasley said after the game. "But I'm glad we ate up some clock, because we spent a lot of time fumbling the ball out here and getting penalties and putting ourselves in harm's way on more than one occasion."

K-State had just one turnover, but fumbled three times. Beasley was also sacked twice. But it was the Wildcats' Lamar Chapman who made the biggest defensive play of the game. He stepped in front of Washington's Gerald Harris and intercepted a pass on the goal-line and returned it eight yards, ending a huge Huskie threat. From there Beasley led K-State down the field on its long drive, and scored the game-winning touchdown himself on a one-yard run.

Quincy Morgan was the Cats' top receiver, and Beasley led all K-State runners. The Wildcats finished with 354 yards of total offense.

The win gave K-State its third straight 11-win season.

1. How many touchdowns did Beasley score in the game?

2. How many yards rushing did Beasley have in the game?

3. How receiving yards did K-State's Quincy Morgan have?

4. How many turnovers did Washington have in the game?

5. Jamie Rheem kicked a field goal in the second quarter. How far was it?

6. How many sacks did K-State have in the game?

7. What was K-State's final ranking in the polls?

Mark Simoneau tackles Washington quarterback Marques Tuiasosopo.

Jonathan Beasley carries the ball during the 1999 Holiday Bowl.

Stadiums

Stadiums are an important part of a team's existence, and usually reflect the successes of a program. Kansas State's KSU Stadium/Wagner Field provides a thriving, exuberant atmosphere on Wildcat game days, presenting the festivity of college football at its best. While KSU has always had supportive, loyal fans, the past 10 years of success in the program provided the catalyst to renovate, refurbish and expand it into the wonderful facility it is today. The stadium, when packed with purple-clad fans, is truly one of the showcase pieces of the Big 12 Conference.

Memorial Stadium

Kansas State has primarily used three different football fields for its home games since the school began playing the sport. After playing informally in Manhattan City Park, the school was granted permission by the city of Manhattan to play its games at the public square bounded by Eighth and Vattier Streets, and Bluemont and Juliette Avenues in 1897. A roofed grandstand was added to the field in May, 1901, and a new grandstand went up in 1906.

In 1910 the Board of Regents voted to build an athletic field on the southwest corner of campus, and the first football game was played there in the fall of 1911. In 1919 the concept of building a new stadium was combined with building a memorial to the 45 K-State students who died during World War I. And so in May, 1922, construction began on the west side of the stadium, at the same location as the standing field.

Action at Ahearn Field in 1917.

Memorial Stadium in the early stages of its construction.

Memorial Stadium was used by the K-State football team for 46 seasons, through the 1967 season.

1. What was the name of K-State's first football field?

2. What was the second field (the first on campus) called?

3. Who did K-State play in the first official game at Memorial Stadium?

Memorial Stadium

4. What was the original capacity of the stadium supposed to be?

5. When was the east side of the stadium completed?

6. Memorial Stadium was originally planned to be in what shape?

7. Why weren't the original plans completed at Memorial Stadium?

8. Who did K-State play in its final game at Memorial Stadium?

9. Who was the last KSU football player to score at Memorial Stadium?

KSU Stadium/Wagner Field

With the ever-increasing popularity of college football in the 1960s, it was soon determined K-State needed to upgrade its football stadium and other athletic facilities. And KSU Stadium was born. Financed

Artist's rendering of KSU Stadium before it was built.

from student fees, athletic gate receipts and contributions, the Wildcats played their first game in the new stadium at the beginning of the 1968 season.

The stadium has been upgraded several times during the past 30 years; additions have included 4,000 permanent seats and 3,000 temporary seats in 1970. The office/dressing room complex at the north end of the stadium was added in 1972. The JumboTron Screen, new scoreboards and marquis message board were added to the complex in 1996. The most recent expansion followed the 1998 season and included another 8,000 permanent seats, a club seating area and 31 additional sky suites. The capacity of KSU Stadium/Wagner Field is now more than 50,000.

KSU Stadium in the 1970s.

KSU Stadium/Wagner Field in 1999.

1. What was the original cost of KSU Stadium?

2. Who did K-State play in the first game at KSU Stadium?

3. What was the original seating capacity of KSU Stadium?

4. When was Astroturf first installed at the stadium?

5. When were the permanent lights added to the field?

6. When was "Wagner Field" added to the name of the stadium?

7. When was the new press box added to the stadium?

8. What is the largest crowd to see a game at KSU Stadium?

Conferences

1. When did K-State first join the Missouri Valley Conference?

2. When was the Big Six Conference formed?

3. Who were the original six schools in the Big Six?

4. Which school joined the Big Six to make it the Big Seven?

5. Which school joined the Big Seven to make it the Big Eight?

6. How many conference championships have the Wildcats won in football?

7. Four Texas schools joined the Big Eight to form the Big 12 Conference. What was the name of the conference they came from?

8. Who are the four schools from Texas?

Quarterbacks

1. Who was K-State's quarterback on the 1934 Big Six championship team?

2. This quarterback was the first of five different K-State quarterbacks to throw four touchdown passes in a game. He did it against Louisiana Tech in 1988. Who is he?

3. This quarterback threw four touchdown passes in a game four different times. Who is he?

4. This quarterback led the Wildcats in passing four straight years, from 1979-82. Who is he?

5. Who was K-State's "quarter" in the Wildcats' first win over KU?

6. Kansas State was 7-3 and just missed going to the Orange Bowl in 1954. Who was the team's quarterback that season?

7. Who took over the Wildcats' quarterbacking duties when Lynn Dickey graduated?

8. Who was the first K-State quarterback to pass for 1,000 yards in a season?

Dennis Morrison

9. Two Wildcat quarterbacks have passed for more than 2,000 yards in a season twice. Who are they?

Running Backs

1. How many Wildcat running backs have rushed for over 1,000 yards in a single season?

2. Who holds the single-game record for most yards gained?

3. This back averaged a whopping 7.3 yards per carry in route to running for 529 yards in 1954. Who is he?

4. Who holds the record for the most rushing attempts in a game?

5. Four different K-State running backs have reached the 200-yard rushing mark in a single game. Who are they?

6. Only one back has been the Wildcats' rushing leader for three different seasons. Who is he?

7. This back was the team's leading rusher and receiver in 1969. Who is he?

8. Four different backs ran for more than 2,000 yards during their careers for K-State. Who are they?

9. This running back ran for more than 100 yards in six consecutive games during the 1973 season. Who is he?

10. Who holds the record for the most 100-yard rushing games in a career at K-State?

11. Who holds the K-State record for the longest run from scrimmage?

Corky Taylor

Receivers

1. Who holds the K-State record for the most pass receptions in a game?

2. Who was the first Wildcat receiver to finish a season with 1,000 receiving yards?

3. Four different players have caught 12 passes in a game for K-State. Who are they?

4. Who holds the K-State record for the most receptions in a season?

5. Who was the first Wildcat receiver to record 100 yards in pass receiving for a single game?

6. Kevin Lockett is the all-time leader for K-State in touchdown receptions with 26. Who is second in school history?

7. Who holds K-State's single-game record for the most yards receiving?

8. Four K-State receivers have caught three touchdown passes in a game. Who are they?

9. This receiver had 188 yards receiving against Nebraska in 1968, the most by a K-State player against a conference opponent. Who is he?

10. This future basketball coach was the team leader in receptions with 14 in 1956. Who is he?

Darnell McDonald

Defense

1. Who is K-State's all-time leader in tackles?

2. This player returned an interception 100 yards for a touchdown against Missouri in 1996. Who is he?

3. Lyle Koontz led the Wildcats with six interceptions in 1949. Hi Faubion picked off six passes in 1951. K-State didn't have a player with six interceptions in a season again until 1985. Who was that player?

Brooks Barta

4. Who holds the season sack record for K-State?

5. Who holds the single-game record at K-State for most tackles?

6. Who holds the Wildcats' season and career records for most tackles for a loss?

7. K-State held an opponent to one first down in a game in 1939. Who was the opponent?

8. Twice in the school's history the Wildcats have picked off seven passes in a game, and both times it was against the same team. Who was the opponent?

9. This player returned a fumble 67 yards (a school record) for a touchdown against Kansas in 1924 to provide the winning margin over the Jayhawks in K-State's 6-0 win. Who was the player?

10. K-State once posted four straight shutouts over opponents, a school record. In what season did the Wildcat defense perform this amazing feat?

Danny Lankas

Kickers

1. Three K-State players hold the record for the most punts in a game. Who are they?

2. Who holds the record for the longest punt in K-State history, a 93-yard boot against Nebraska in 1980?

3. Two kickers have made 60-yard plus field goals for K-State. Who are they?

4. Martin Gramatica is the all-time leading field-goal kicker in K-State history, connecting 54 times for three points. Two kickers have made 37 field goals for the Wildcats. Who are they?

5. Who was the first K-State kicker to make a 50-yard field goal?

6. Jamie Rheem and Martin Gramatica hold the school record with the most extra points made in a game with nine. Who held the previous record of eight?

7. Who holds the K-State record for career punting average?

8. Who holds the K-State record for the most punts in a career?

9. Who holds the single-game record for highest average per punt?

Mark Porter

Uniform Numbers

1. How many numbers have been retired by K-State?

2. What was Eric Gallon's number?

3. What was Eric Hickson's number?

4. What number did receiver Dave Jones wear as a Wildcat?

5. What number did linebacker Dan Lankas wear?

6. What number did running back Isaac Jackson wear?

7. What number did quarterback Darrell Dickey wear?

8. What numbers did Andre Coleman wear?

9. What number did Ralph Graham wear as a Wildcat?

10. What number did Gerald Hackney wear for the Wildcats?

11. What was Reggie Singletary's number at K-State?

12. What was J. J. Smith's number?

Rivalries

K-State – KU game in 1936.

1. Which school has K-State played the most in its football history?

2. K-State used to play this team every year on Thanksgiving Day. Who was the rival team?

3. When was the first K-State-KU football game?

4. When did K-State record its first win over the Jayhawks?

5. Which school has K-State defeated the most times?

6. Which school has K-State lost to the most times?

7. In the past six seasons Nebraska has become one of K-State's top rivals. After losing many years in a row to the Huskers, KSU defeated Nebraska in 1998. When did K-State last defeat the Huskers before 1998, and what was the score?

8. What is the name of the trophy K-State and KU play for each year?

9. The Wildcats currently own a seven-game winning streak (through the 1999 season) against Kansas. What was previously the longest winning streak against the Jayhawks?

What Position Did He Play?

Name the primary position for each of the players listed.

Bill Butler

1. Quentin Neujahr

2. Dirk Ochs

3. Bill Butler

4. Mario Smith

5. Joe Gordon

6. Tim Colston

7. Willis Crenshaw

8. Maurice Henry

9. Jarrod Cooper

10. Barton Hundley

The NFL Draft

1. Who was the first K-State player drafted by an NFL team?

2. Who was the first K-State player chosen in the first round of the NFL Draft?

3. Who were the first K-Staters selected in the AFL (American Football League) Draft?

4. Two defensive backs from K-State have been selected in the first round of the NFL Draft. Who are they?

5. Who was the first K-State quarterback drafted by an NFL team?

6. The most K-State players selected in a single NFL draft is seven. What year was this record number of Wildcats selected?

7. Who was the first Bill Snyder coached player to be drafted by an NFL team?

8. In which round of the 1996 Draft was Percell Gaskins selected?

9. Only one K-State player was selected in the 1998 NFL Draft. Who is he?

10. In which round of the 1999 Draft was wide receiver Darnell McDonald selected?

11. Which K-State player was selected in the highest round of the 2000 NFL Draft?

In the Pros

1. Who was the first K-State player to play professional football?

2. Who were the first two K-State players to play for a CFL (Canadian Football League) team?

3. What team did running back Larry Brown play for in the NFL?

4. Running back Don Calhoun finished his pro career in 1984 with which pro team?

5. Elmer Hackney played for three different NFL teams. Who were the teams he played for?

Kevin Lockett

6. Richard Sears played for Kansas City's first NFL team in 1924. What was the name of that team?

7. Chad May played one season in the World League. What team did he play for?

8. Mack Herron started his pro career with which CFL team?

9. Barrett Brooks played for the Philadelphia Eagles from 1995-1998. Which team did he play for in 1999?

10. After playing with the Packers and Chiefs, which team did Paul Coffman finish his NFL career with?

Smart Guys

Stan Weber

1. Who was K-State's first Academic All-Big Eight player in football?

2. This future Wildcat head football coach was K-State's first Academic All-American in 1956. Who is he?

3. Who was the first two-time Academic All-American from K-State?

4. This Wildcat is the only quarterback from K-State to earn Academic All-American honors. Who is he?

5. Who was selected as K-State's first Outstanding Scholar-Athlete in 1989?

6. This wide receiver was first-team Academic All-Big Eight three times, and first-team Academic All-Big 12 once. Who is he?

7. This K-State punter was a two-time Academic All-American in 1985 and 1986. Who is he?

8. This offensive guard was an Academic All-American in 1987. Who is he?

Miscellaneous

1. Who is the only Wildcat head coach to become a head coach of an NFL team?

2. Who was the first K-State player to play in the Super Bowl?

3. Kansas State has used three different mascot names for its athletic teams. What are the three different names?

4. The Big Eight Conference began selecting Players of the Week in 1971. Who was the first K-State player to receive this award?

5. Which year did K-State's offensive players wear different color helmets for one season; the ends and backs wore white helmets, and the linemen wore purple helmets?

6. Two Kansas State head coaches have been inducted into the National College Football Hall of Fame. Who are they?

Trivia Answers

An air bound Percell Gaskins attempts to block a field goal.

Trivia Answers

Wildcats Players Trivia

Michael Bishop

1. Blinn Community College
2. None. Blinn CC was 22-0 when he was the starter.
3. Davey O'Brien Award as the nation's top quarterback
4. 2,844
5. 23
6. 14
7. 748
8. Northeast Louisiana. He also had four touchdown passes in the game.
9. Ricky Williams of Texas
10. Aaron Lockett, against Northeast Louisiana
11. New England Patriots, in the seventh round

Chris Canty

1. quarterback
2. Jim Thorpe
3. three
4. two
5. one
6. 14
7. once, in 1996
8. first round by New England

Lynn Dickey

1. Osawatomie, Kansas
2. 29
3. 994

4. three
5. 64
6. 6,208
7. twice, 1969 and 1970
8. third round by Houston Oilers
9. Houston and Green Bay

Steve Grogan

1. Ottawa, Kansas
2. 2,213
3. 12
4. 1,143
5. six
6. 14
7. fifth round by New England
8. Just one, the Patriots

Kevin Lockett

1. Booker T. Washington High School
2. Michael Smith
3. 26
4. 72
5. Biletnikoff Award, presented annually to the nation's outstanding receiver
6. 217
7. second round
8. 81

Jaime Mendez

1. Cardinal Mooney High School in Youngstown, Ohio
2. six
3. 15
4. three times, 1991-93
5. one, in 1990
6. He wasn't drafted.
7. He played part of the season with the Philadelphia Eagles.
8. Baltimore

Gary Spani

1. Manhattan High School
2. three times, 1975-77
3. 543
4. UPI, Kodak, *Football News* and *Kickoff Magazine*
5. Danny Lankas had 178 stops in 1967.
6. third round
7. Kansas City Chiefs
8. 10

Percell Gaskins

1. Seabreeze High in Daytona Beach, Florida
2. Northwest Oklahoma State
3. high jump
4. once, in 1995
5. 258
6. St. Louis Rams
7. two, St. Louis and Carolina

Ralph Graham

1. El Dorado, Kansas
2. Basketball. He was All-Big Six his senior year.
3. Wichita (Wichita State today) and Notre Dame
4. 31
5. 13
6. He was the head coach at Wichita in 1942, 1946-47. His record was 17-13.
7. The Raisin Bowl, in Fresno, California. Wichita lost to Pacific, 26-14.
8. 4-26-1

Martin Gramatica

1. Argentina
2. "Automatica"
3. 54
4. .771. He made 54 of 70 kicks.
5. 65 yards against Northern Illinois on September 12, 1998
6. 135
7. 349 points
8. The Lou Groza Award, presented to the nation's top kicker. He was the runner-up in 1998.
9. Tampa Bay

Veryl Switzer

1. Bogue High School in Nicodemus, Kansas
2. long jump
3. defensive back
4. three, one in 1952 and two in 1953
5. 31.0
6. eight

7. Drake
8. Green Bay Packers

Henry Cronkite

1. KU
2. basketball and track
3. UPI, *New York Sun*, *New York World-Telegram*, NEA, *Illustrated Football Annual*, Frank O'Neill, *New York Journal*, Charles Parker, College Humor, and Dr. Lacy Lockert
4. end
5. twice, in 1930 and 1931
6. Brooklyn Dodgers

Elmer Hackney

1. "One Man Gang," "Maharajah of Might," and "Mr. Muscle"
2. They were canceled because of World War II.
3. twice, in 1937 and 1938
4. He injured his knee.
5. 11th round
6. Philadelphia Eagles
7. Three: Philadelphia, Pittsburgh and Detroit
8. 846. He also scored 12 touchdowns.

Ray Hahn

1. Clay Center
2. To serve in the Student Army Training Corps.
3. Grantland Rice All-American team
4. Hammond Pros
5. Norton Community High School
6. basketball

Cornelius Davis

1. Corny
2. 1,873
3. 20
4. 172 yards against Cincinnati on October 22, 1966
5. none
6. Minnesota Vikings

Mack Herron

1. Hutchinson (Kansas) Community College
2. 21
3. 815
4. 26.2
5. 52 receptions for 652 yards
6. sixth round by the Atlanta Falcons
7. Winnipeg Blue Bombers of the CFL
8. two, New England and Atlanta

Clarence Scott

1. Trinity High School in Decatur, Georgia
2. wide receiver
3. four
4. one, in 1968
5. first, by the Cleveland Browns
6. Just one, the Browns
7. 39

Andre Coleman

1. Hickory High in Hermitage, Pennsylvania
2. none
3. two, against New Mexico State in 1993, and against Wyoming in the 1993 Copper Bowl
4. 1,556
5. 12
6. San Diego Chargers
7. three: San Diego, Seattle and Pittsburgh

Mark Simoneau

1. three times, 1997-99
2. four: two in '98 and two in '99
3. 400
4. Chris Canty in 1994 and Travis Ochs in 1995
5. twice, in 1998 and 1999
6. third round by the Atlanta Falcons

Reggie Singletary

1. Cowley County (Kansas)Community College
2. 281
3. 60, for minus-298 yards
4. linebacker
5. three times, 1981-83
6. He wasn't drafted and never played in the pros.

Sean Snyder

1. 1988 Peach Bowl when he was at Iowa
2. 43.0
3. once, in 1992
4. 80

5. Blue-Gray Game and the Senior Bowl
6. Phoenix

Chad May

1. Cal State - Fullerton
2. 5,253
3. 34
4. 15
5. two
6. Minnesota

George Maddox

1. Buster
2. Greenville, Texas
3. The All-America Board, Bill Corum and the Illustrated Football Annual. He was a second-team pick by Dr. Lacy Lockert.
4. three
5. Green Bay
6. one, in 1935

David Allen

1. Liberty, Missouri
2. 16.7, going into 2000 season
3. none
4. 22.1
5. 553, going into 2000 season
6. 16: seven rushing, two receiving and seven on punt returns, going into 2000 season
7. twice, 1998-99

More Wildcat Trivia

Bill Snyder

1. William Jewell
2. Missouri and California
3. North Texas State, 1976-78, under Fry. Snyder went to Iowa with Fry in 1979.
4. Oklahoma State in 1990. KSU beat the Cowboys 23-17 in Manhattan.
5. defensive back
6. ESPN honored Coach Snyder with its Coach of the Year Award in 1991.
7. Eastern New Mexico, in 1963 as a graduate assistant
8. 88-40-1
9. 31
10. Two. He was the head coach at Indio High School in California, and at Foothill High School in Santa Ana, California

Vince Gibson

1. 33-52
2. one, 1970
3. twice, in 1969 and 1972
4. second place, in 1970
5. 12th, the week of November 1, 1969. KSU lost to Mizzou that week and dropped to 15th.
6. He defeated Oklahoma State, Colorado and Iowa State three times each.

Jim Dickey

1. 25-53-2
2. Air Force, 34-21, in Dickey's fourth game as head coach
3. three times: in 1978, 1982 and 1984
4. Colorado, four times: in 1978, 1980, 1982 and 1984
5. none
6. Wichita State, 16-10 in Manhattan

Charles Bachman

1. Notre Dame
2. Great Lakes Naval Station. This team won the 1919 Rose Bowl.
3. Michigan State
4. five: 1921-23, 1925-26
5. Hillsdale College
6. 33-23-9

Other Coaches

1. Ira Pratt
2. Mike Ahearn. His career record at K-State was 39-12.
3. Bill Meek
4. Hobbs Adams in 1946 and Sam Francis in 1947
5. K-State finished 7-2-1 in 1934 and won the Big Six Conference
6. Oklahoma A&M
7. Northwestern
8. Lee Moon. His record was 1-8.
9. Just one, Kansas, 29-12 in 1986.
10. Kansas

Bowl Games

1982 Independence Bowl

1. Kilisimasi Toluao, with 31 yards on 10 carries

2. The Badgers lost three fumbles to KSU.

3. 127. He completed 13 of 35 pass attempts with one interception.

4. Dan Ruzich and Stu Peters both finished the game with 10 stops.

5. Randy Wright. He had touchdown tosses of 16 and 87 yards.

6. two: one fumble and one interception

7. The announced attendance was 49,523. Because of the poor weather, the actual attendance was less than half that total.

1993 Copper Bowl

1. Seven: J. J. Smith, Tate Wright, Chad May, Andre Coleman, Kevin Lockett, Leon Edwards and Kenny McEntyre

2. 275. He hit 19 of 28 pass attempts.

3. Two: 61-yarder to Andre Coleman in the third period and a 30-yard strike to Kevin Lockett in the third period.

4. 133 on 20 carries

5. Laird Veatch, with 13 stops

6. On a 68-yard punt return

7. Kenny McEntyre

8. 502

9. Andre Coleman. He had 283 yards of total offense (144 receiving, seven rushing, 73 punt return yards and 59 yards on kickoff returns). He also scored two touchdowns.

10. Three times

1994 Aloha Bowl

1. minus-61 yards

2. eight

3. Joe Gordon blocked a punt into the end zone. Chris Sublette recovered the ball for the score.

4. Kevin Lockett had five receptions for 99 yards.

5. Punter Eric Hardy averaged 45.5 yards on 11 punts.

6. Joe Gordon

1995 Holiday Bowl

1. Miller completed 6 of 8 passes for 82 yards

2. Four: 12 yards to Brian Lojka, 18 yards to Tyson Schwieger, four yards to Kevin Lockett and 33 yards to Mitch Running.

3. 536 total yards, 212 rushing and 324 passing

4. 103 on 20 carries

5. Mario Smith had two and Steve Hanks had one

6. 126 yards on six receptions. He scored one touchdown.

1997 Cotton Bowl

1. Andre Anderson on a 41-yard pass from Kavanagh
2. 72 yards
3. eight
4. eight
5. Mike Lawrence had 23 carries for 54 yards
6. Mike Lawrence
7. Kevin Lockett for K-State and Steve Sarkisian for BYU
8. 135 on seven receptions

1997 Fiesta Bowl

1. four: 19 yards to McDonald, 28 yards to Justin Swift, 77 yards to McDonald and 41 yards to McDonald
2. 206 on seven receptions. He scored three touchdowns.
3. Bishop had 77 yards on 15 carries
4. Bishop, on a 12-yard run in the second quarter
5. none
6. Demetric Denmark made nine stops

1998 Alamo Bowl

1. David Allen ran for 83 yards on 13 carries
2. Darnell McDonald, who caught five passes for 124 yards and two touchdowns
3. Jake Havick recovered a fumble in the end zone
4. 53, and completed 25
5. three
6. twice
7. five on 24 rushing attempts

1999 Culligan Holiday Bowl

1. three
2. 48 on 20 carries
3. 104 on eight receptions
4. two: one fumble and one interception
5. 41 yards
6. five, for minus-27 yards
7. sixth, the highest season-ending ranking in school history

Stadiums

Memorial Stadium

1. It didn't have an official name, but was referred to as the Athletic Field.
2. Ahearn Field, named after Mike Ahearn, the school's athletic director at the time and former football coach
3. Washburn, on October 6, 1922. K-State won the game 47-0.
4. 22,500
5. 1924
6. A horseshoe
7. The Great Depression hit and the plans were dropped to enclose the south end zone.
8. Colorado, who defeated the Wildcats 40-6
9. Cornelius Davis scored from a yard out in the third quarter against Colorado in the last home game of the 1967 season. Colorado scored the final touchdown at Memorial Stadium, a fourth-quarter touchdown by Dan Kelly in the Buffaloes' 40-6 victory.

KSU Stadium/ Wagner Field

1. $1.6 million
2. Colorado State on September 21, 1968. KSU won the game, 21-0.
3. 35,000
4. 1970
5. 1983
6. 1991, in honor of Dave and Carol Wagner of Dodge City
7. 1993
8. A record crowd of 52,254 saw the Wildcats devour the Jayhawks, 50-9, on October 9, 1999.

Conferences

1. 1913. The school applied for admission to the conference in 1911.
2. 1929 was the first year of the Big Six.
3. K-State, Kansas, Nebraska, Iowa State, Missouri and Oklahoma
4. Colorado
5. Oklahoma State
6. one, in 1934
7. Southwest Conference
8. Texas, Texas A&M, Baylor and Texas Tech

Quarterbacks

1. Leo Ayers, who was selected as first-team All-Big Six by three different sources
2. Paul Watson

3. Brian Kavanagh, against Colorado State in 1995, and Rice, Oklahoma and Kansas in 1996.
4. Darrell Dickey
5. Roy Graves
6. Jim Logsdon
7. Dennis Morrison, who led the K-State offense in 1971-72
8. Bill Nossek, with 1,220 in 1967
9. Lynn Dickey and Chad May

Running Backs

1. Four. J.J. Smith (1994), Eric Gallon (1991), Isaac Jackson (1973), and Cornelius Davis (1966).
2. Mike Lawrence, 252 yards rushing against Iowa State on November 23, 1996
3. Corky Taylor
4. Bill Butler, 41 against BYU on September 25, 1971
5. Mike Lawrence, 252 yards against Iowa State on November 23, 1996; J. J. Smith, 227 yards against UNLV on November 26, 1994; Tony Jordan, 218 yards against Iowa State on November 15, 1986; and L. J. Brown, 200 yards against Air Force on September 29, 1979
6. Eric Hickson, who led in 1995 with 816 yards rushing, 1997 with 750 yards, and 1998 with 902 yards
7. Mack Herron
8. Eric Hickson (2,537 yards), Mike Lawrence (2,265 yards), J. J. Smith (2,210 yards), and Isaac Jackson (2,182 yards)
9. Isaac Jackson

10. J. J. Smith and Eric Hickson, 10 each
11. Gerald Hackney ripped off a 96-yard touchdown run against Kansas in 1948.

Receivers

1. Michael Smith caught 13 passes against Missouri on October 21, 1989.
2. Darnell McDonald, who finished the 1998 season with 1,092 receiving yards
3. Darnell McDonald against Nebraska in 1998, Kevin Lockett against Oklahoma in 1996, Michael Smith against Washington in 1991, and Mack Herron against Colorado in 1969
4. Darnell McDonald, 75 in 1998
5. Dick Johnson, who totaled 150 yards in receiving against Tulsa in 1949
6. Darnell McDonald with 15
7. Darnell McDonald, with 206 yards receiving against Syracuse in the 1997 Fiesta Bowl
8. John Williams, against Austin Peay State in 1987; Michael Smith, against Iowa State in 1991; Jimmy Dean, against Rice in 1996; and Darnell McDonald, against Syracuse in the 1997 Fiesta Bowl
9. Dave Jones
10. Gene Keady, who has been highly successful at Purdue as the Boilermakers' head basketball coach

Defense

1. Gary Spani, with 543 tackles
2. Mario Smith
3. Barton Hundley had six picks in the 1985 season
4. Nyle Wiren, with 11.5 in 1996
5. Danny Lankas made an incredible 28 tackles against Missouri on November 11, 1967
6. Reggie Singletary. He made 28 tackles for losses in 1981 and finished his career with a total of 60.
7. Colorado
8. Missouri. K-State picked off seven against the Tigers on October 8, 1938 and November 17, 1951.
9. Don Meek
10. 1933. KSU defeated KU 6-0, tied Michigan State 0-0, beat Iowa State 7-0, and defeated Oklahoma 14-0.

Kickers

1. George Carter, against Missouri in 1951; John Drew, against Missouri in 1961; and Bob Coble, against Missouri in 1968
2. Don Birdsey
3. Martin Gramatica made a 65-yard field goal against Northern Illinois in 1998 and Mark Porter kicked a 61-yarder against Nebraska in 1988.
4. Steve Willis (1981-84) and Mark Porter (1985-88)
5. Max Arreguin made a 50-yard field goal against Nebraska on November 11, 1968

6. Jamie Rheem, who made eight extra-point attempts against Indiana State on September 7, 1996
7. James Garcia, who averaged 43.2 yards per punt on 167 punts (1995-98)
8. Don Birdsey punted the ball 283 times during his career from 1977-1980
9. James Garcia averaged 60.3 yards per punt on four kicks against Texas in 1998

Uniform Numbers

1. One, number 11, honoring Lynn Dickey and Steve Grogan
2. 1
3. 24
4. 81
5. 33
6. 25
7. 4
8. 2 and 28
9. 61
10. 66
11. 98
12. 22

Rivalries

1. Kansas. K-State and KU have met 97 times on the gridiron.
2. Washburn University in Topeka, Kansas
3. 1902. KU won the game in Lawrence, 16-0.
4. 1906. The Aggies won the game, 6-4.
5. Iowa State. K-State has defeated the Cyclones 33 times.
6. Nebraska. The Cornhuskers have defeated the Wildcats 71 times.
7. 1968 in Lincoln, 12-0
8. The Governor's Cup, which is presented to the winning team by the Governor of Kansas. The trophy resides with the winning team each season.
9. Four games, from 1924 through 1927

What Position Did He Play?

1. center
2. defensive end
3. fullback
4. strong safety
5. cornerback
6. defensive tackle
7. fullback
8. defensive end
9. strong safety
10. free safety

The NFL Draft

1. Maurice Elder, by the Boston Redskins in 1937
2. Veryl Switzer, by the Green Bay Packers in 1954. He was the third overall selection in the draft.
3. John Littleton, by the Buffalo Bills; and Joe Vader, by the Dallas Texans
4. Clarence Scott, selected by Cleveland in 1971, and Chris Canty, taken by New England in 1997
5. Lynn Dickey, in the third round of the 1971 draft by Houston
6. 1974: Henry Childs fifth round, Willie Cullars seventh, Don Calhoun 10th, Bill Brittain 11th, Fred Rothwell 13th, John Wells 15th, and Isaac Jackson 15th
7. Maurice Henry, in the sixth round of the 1990 draft by Detroit
8. Fourth round, by the Rams
9. Todd Weiner, by Seattle in the second round
10. Seventh round by Tampa Bay
11. Darren Howard, in the second round by New Orleans

In the Pros

1. Alvin Jolley, for the Akron Pros in 1922
2. Joe Blanchard and Rollin Prather, who both played for the Edmonton Eskimos from 1950-1954
3. Washington Redskins, 1969-76
4. New Jersey Generals of the USFL
5. Philadelphia Eagles (1940), Pittsburgh Steelers (1941) and Detroit Lions (1942-46)
6. Cowboys
7. Frankfort Galaxy in 1997
8. Winnipeg Blue Bombers (1970-72)
9. Detroit Lions
10. Minnesota Vikings in 1988

Smart Guys

1. Frank Rodman, in 1954. He was also selected in 1955.
2. Ellis Rainsberger
3. Floyd Dorsey. He was selected in 1975 and 1977.
4. Stan Weber. He was selected in 1984.
5. Brooks Barta. He was also honored in 1992, and was a first-team Academic All-American in 1992 as well.
6. Kevin Lockett
7. Troy Faunce
8. Matt Garver

Miscellaneous

1. Bo McMillin, who led K-State to a record of 29-21-1. He went to the Detroit Lions in 1948.
2. Offensive lineman Lynn Larson played for the Baltimore Colts when they took on the Dallas Cowboys in Super Bowl V.
3. Aggies, used until 1915; Wildcats, used in 1915 and from 1920 to the present; and Farmers, used from 1916 to 1919.
4. Junior quarterback Dennis Morrison was chosen after his great performance against Oklahoma State on November 6, 1971. He completed 23 of 43 passes for 303 yards and three touchdowns as K-State defeated the Cowboys, 35-23.
5. 1947. The NCAA stopped the practice the following year.
6. Lynn "Pappy" Waldorf was the first inductee in 1966. Charlie Bachman was inducted in 1978.

Photo Credits

Courtesy of Kansas State University Sports Information - 14, 16, 20 bottom, 25, 27, 29, 35, 51, 55, 56, 58 top, 59-61, 63-65, 70, 74 top, 76, 80, 81, 84-86, 88-90, 93, 94 top left, 96, 98-100, 104, 106, 108, 110, 112, 114, 116, 118, 120, 122, 124, 126, 128, 130, 132, 134, 136, 138, 140, 142, 144, 146, 160, 162, 164-166, 168, 170, 172, 174, 176, 179, 183, 185, 189, 190, 195, 197-200, 203, 205, 206, 208, 210, back cover bottom

Kansas State University Photographic Services - 19, 26, 28, 31-32, 34, 44, 47, 69 bottom, 77 left, 78, 79, 87, 91, 94 bottom, 176, 181, 191

Kansas State University Archives - 20 (logos)

The University of Kansas Archives, Kenneth Spencer Library - 17, 18 bottom, 23, 24, 38, 43, 48, 49, 53, 54, 58 bottom, 66-68, 77 right, 102, 188, 202, back cover top and middle

The University of Kansas Archives, Kenneth Spencer Library, *Lawrence Journal-World* Collection - 18 top, 22, 58 bottom, 69 top, 71, 74 bottom, 82, 193, 208

Pete Aiken - 94 top right, 187

About the Author

Mark Stallard is a free-lance writer who lives in Overland Park, Kansas, with his wife Merrie Jo. He has written for *The Wichita Eagle* and has had his work appear in several publications. *Wildcats to Powercats* is Mark's fourth book.